ANTIQUE COLLECTING IN THE MIDWEST

Antique Collecting

IN THE

MIDWEST

Sara Simonsgaard

with

MARGUERITE BOOKSTEIN

Illustrated by

MARKIE McRAE

CHICAGO REVIEW PRESS

First Edition
First Printing 1976

Published by
Chicago Review Press, Incorporated
811 West Junior Terrace
Chicago, Illinois 60613

ISBN (paperbound edition) 0-914090-21-6

Library of Congress Catalog Number 76-41614

The section of the map shown on the cover was taken from "Mitchell's Traveller's Guide Through the United States", Philadelphia: Mitchell & Hinman, No. 6 North 5th Street. 1837.

Book design and typography by Claire J. Mahoney

Chicago Review Press Books are distributed by
The Swallow Press Incorporated
811 West Junior Terrace
Chicago, Illinois 60613

If this book is not avaliable at your local bookstore, CHICAGO REVIEW PRESS will mail you a copy, postage prepaid, upon receipt of your name, address and payment of $5.95.

To the memory of my beloved husband Jules Simonsgaard

Contents

PART II

Illustrations

Acknowledgements

The most enjoyable part of writing this book is in thanking the people whose help made it possible. These people include museum curators and librarians, auctioneers and dealers in antiques, managers of antique shows, representatives of collectors groups, and collectors of antiques:

Milo M. Neave, Curator of American Arts, The Art Institute of Chicago

John W. Keefe, Curator of European Decorative Arts, The Art Institute of Chicago

Ruth R. Philbrick, Head of Photographic Archives, The National Gallery, Washington, D.C.

Annette Fern, Architecture Librarian, Ryerson & Burnham Libraries, The Art Institute of Chicago

Carolyn Hurt, Librarian — Reference Department, Ryerson & Burnham Libraries, The Art Institute of Chicago

Marshall Field & Company

Joseph W. Fell

Nancy Frahm

Paul Mark Franklin

Donald C. Koehn

Elaine Luartes

Nadine P. Martens

Beverley R. Milne

Myrna Mohler

Kenneth Nebenzahl

Virginia W. Packer

Opal Sallee

Laurence Schaberg

Susan Tanner

Holly Wesley

And of course I wish to thank all the dealers who answered my letters asking for their listings; and to express my regrets to those dealers whose replies I did not receive because of the poor functioning of the U.S. Postal Service.

Jean Crutcher gave me great help and encouragement. Lester Shawver contributed substantially to the chapter on the Midwest market. Abraham Bookstein made many helpful suggestions about the text. Terry Dunning, President of the National Auctioneers Association, took time from one of the busiest years of his life to help me.

The editorial expertise of Marguerite Bookstein, her concern for the book as a whole and her meticulous attention to detail was indispensable. She has my heartfelt thanks.

The quality of Markie McRae's line drawings makes comment superfluous; but not my appreciation and gratitude for her work, which makes our descriptions of various objects more meaningful.

Lastly, I wish to express my thanks to the anonymous collectors and friends who have lent their antiques and collectibles for the drawings and photographs in the book.

Introduction

The purpose of this book is to help Midwestern collectors develop a successful approach to the buying of antiques. It is based on my many years as a collector and dealer in this area, and I have tried to include everything from my experience which might be of use to collectors at all levels.

Part I of the book contains a survey of the types of antiques and collectibles available in the Midwest, a discussion of how to form a collecting strategy, and detailed advice on ways to make the best use of shops, shows, auctions, house sales, books and museums.

Part II of the book consists of carefully selected listings of the various sources for buying antiques, and for finding information about antiques. These sources are well known to me, either by experience or reputation, and they should give satisfaction. I am confident that readers of this book will avoid many costly disappointments, and will soon share my great pleasure in owning beautiful things from the past.

For the sad truth is that the unprepared collector is almost certain to end up with an expensive hodge-podge of items that give little aesthetic satisfaction and do not, as is usual with well-purchased antiques, appreciate in value. How often I have been told, "If only I had started out with a better understanding of the market I would not have wasted all that time and money!" There is no substitute for a systematic approach and solid information. Otherwise your buying will always be a step ahead of your developing taste and expertise, and what looks like a wonderful acquisition one year will seem an embarrassment the next.

Learning quickly is important because antiques and fine collectibles are not becoming more plentiful. Our suggestions should help you get off to a good start with that first important purchase or to move more rapidly in succeeding in a new category. Later will come the knowledge that makes it possible to take advantage of the truly remarkable opportunities that present themselves in the Midwest—such as the time when I went looking for a plain writing table and returned with a Louis XV desk, circa 1760-70. (See illustration, page 15). Really what is necessary is a willingness to cultivate a sense of quality in diverse objects, some knowledge of the antiques market, and the imagination to see that an unexpected find might mix very agreeably with pieces from another period or style.

Of course some money is necessary. Those who say that you can buy a whole houseful of antiques for a song cannot be talking about antiques or fine collectibles at all, but rather about serviceable used furnishings. Although there is nothing at all wrong with such buying, this book is intended for those who desire to collect objects of real aesthetic or historical interest, and such objects are not cheap. But they need not be prohibitively expensive either. As a collector I have had only modest sums at my disposal, and yet by avoiding fads and by aiming for the best within my reach, I have been able to own many fine antiques. These things have proved ever more agreeable with familiarity, and they have given me lasting satisfaction.

There was a time when Midwestern collectors had reason to envy those living in the East which, since it was the part of the country settled first, was long the richest area for both domestic and imported antiques. There is now, however, much less reason for collectors here to envy those in the East. The widespread appreciation of antiques, a feature of eastern life

Louis XV drop-leaf desk, completely covered with marquetry in matched patterns of exotic woods; lighter colored wood on the outside and darker wood on the inside. Made to stand free in a room, the design is a coherent object — a delight when seen from the back or any angle. In today's terminology it would be called plain high style Louis XV, circa 1765–70.

for decades, is still a relatively new phenomenon in the Midwest. Most buyers and sellers are less sophisticated here, and the supply is relatively plentiful. This situation gives the well-prepared collector a fine opportunity, not only to acquire a broad range of antiques at advantageous prices, but also to make the occasional spectacular buy. The Midwest is now a truly diverse and exciting field for the collector and my hope is that readers of this book will gain the confidence and information needed to make the most of it.

PART I

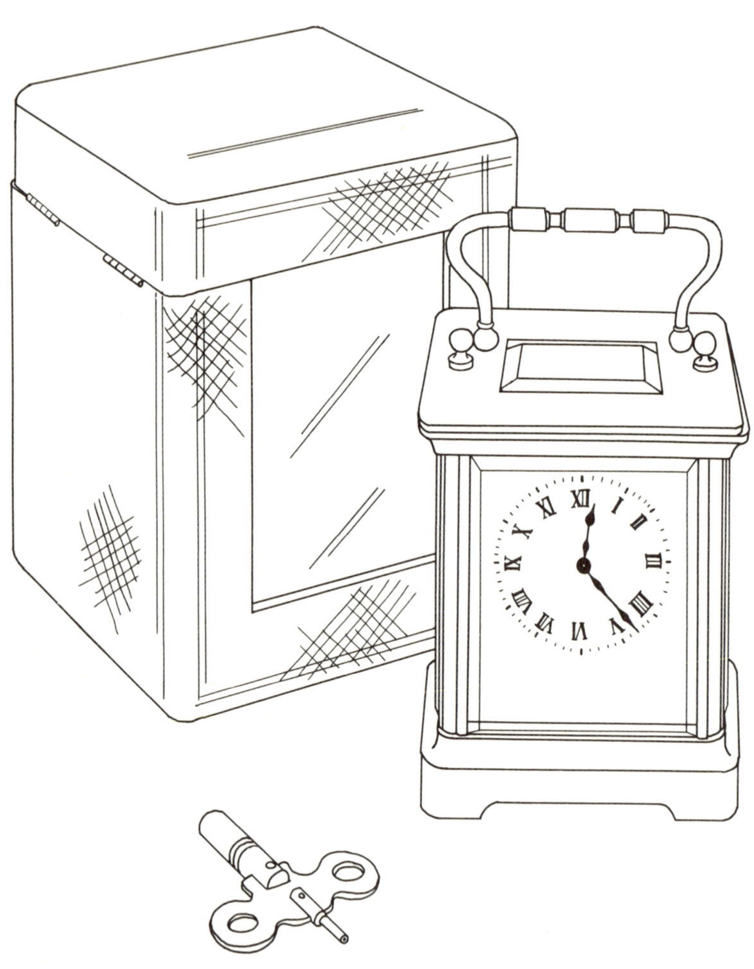

French brass carriage clock, circa 1900. This dainty clock with bevelled glass on all four sides and top, 5⅝″ high to top of handle; retains its velvet-lined, glass-fronted carrying case.

1

COLLECTING:
A Strategy for Success

The field of antiques and collectibles is so vast and complex that you need a systematic approach in order to become a successful and satisfied collector. First, you need to know what the field contains and what is available; otherwise, how can you know what your preferences are? Unless you make an informed decision about what kinds of objects you want to collect, you can easily end up with a hodge-podge of odds and ends that will give you little lasting pleasure, and you will not have learned anything useful from your experience.

Second, once you have decided what objects to collect, you should develop a solid understanding of their characteristics. If you are serious about your collecting, you will want to know such things as when, where, why, and, when possible, by whom these objects were made. Such knowledge will help you in your buying decisions and will give you a better appreciation of the objects you have chosen. A carefully chosen collection is itself a form of art in which you express your taste, knowledge, and personality.

And finally, you must understand the structure of the field of antiques and collectibles, so that you can set goals which are realistic in terms of the objects available and your personal finances.

What is an Antique?

For the purposes of this book, we will define an antique as anything made over one hundred years ago. This is a commonly accepted definition and is taken from a United States customs law which provides that objects over one hundred years old can enter this country without the payment of duty. It is not, however, the only definition. In an earlier law antiques were considered, for purposes of duty, to be objects made before 1830, and this earlier date is still used by some writers to define antiques.

Moreover, you should understand that legal definitions of "antique" are deficient in that they cannot take into account the intrinsic qualities of any given object. To fully qualify as an antique an object must not merely be of a certain age, but must also possess some aesthetic merit; and indeed we would not be so interested in objects from the past if we did not find them lovely. The artistic merit of a given object is dependent on the aesthetic values and methods of craftsmanship particular to the time and place of its making. In this sense, the definition of "antique" varies with the history of the country in question. The periods that have provided the finest antiques from France or England are not the same as those from China, which has had a continuous civilization of more than 3,000 years. Because of the relative youth of the United States, a nation only 200 years old and preceded by less than 175 years as a colony, fine American antiques originate from a comparatively brief period.

Whatever their age or place of origin, prime antiques have always had one attribute in common — the human hand was the dominant instrument in their construction. Because machine construction was common in many trades in the Western world after 1830, many scholars, collectors, and dealers still prefer the 1830 cut-off date, although it is also arbitrary. We have chosen the "one hundred years old" definition for this book because 1) it is more suitable for the Midwest, which was so lately frontier country, and because 2) it is a good way here and now to separate the antiques from the collectibles.

What is a Collectible?

We will define collectibles, as opposed to antiques, simply as all those things made within the last 100 years for the house, farm, or shop, as well as other objects which have been made obsolete by a rapidly developing technology. This category can include collectible objects made today, such as folk art. The field of collectibles includes such things as railroad silver, old drugstore furnishings, limousine flower vases, carnival glass, depression glass, late bottles, the one thousand and one "limited edition" objects of various sorts, and so on and so on. Many objects of this period were produced by machine and, since they can be easily reproduced, you should think carefully before spending substantial amounts of money on them. On the other hand, the quality of workmanship and materials of even a few decades ago makes many collectibles easily worth more than their counterparts made today. With collectibles in particular it is important to learn how to distinguish between quality and mere quaintness.

Newcomers to the field may find the price range in collectibles astonishing. An iron may sell for from $4.00 to $5.00, a washboard for from $3.00 to $4.00. But a Boy Scout cast iron mechanical bank may cost around $900. The price range in glass collectibles is even more striking: a clear depression glass vase in "Manhattan" pattern will cost $2.75, while a Tiffany lamp in "Wisteria" pattern will cost close to $20,000.

The depression glass vase is a completely machine-made product, but the Tiffany lamp required highly skilled handworkmanship. There are of course many more collectibles on the market today than antiques, since collectibles were machine made for a much larger population. What is less obvious is that there are many more *kinds* of collectibles than antiques. Take for example the silver fork. There were very few silver forks in America before 1850, and with rare exceptions these were simply handmade dinner and dessert forks. Three decades later the thirty-five or more varieties available in machine-made sterling and electroplated silver required the use of a chart in order to set a table properly.

Silver dinner and dessert forks made by Edward Edmund Mead, Ithica, New York, circa 1831–32, French thread design. Bought in 1972 at a flea market, $17.50 for each set. Appraised in 1974 at $150 each set.

The Major Categories for Collecting

If we look back over the whole history of decorative arts in the western world, we find that the major categories for collecting — furniture, silver, ceramics and glass — have existed in some form since ancient times. Nonetheless, most of the objects of domestic life that we now collect as antiques were developed in relatively recent times as a byproduct of economic growth and increased political stability. Increased prosperity made possible the adornment of personal life, and as the rulers of Britain and the Continent learned to confine their wars to battlefields rather than ranging freely over the countryside, they and their populations were able to enjoy some of the comforts of a settled home. At the top of society this settling down meant moving from heavily fortified castles into palaces. Lower down on the social scale it meant a much slower movement from huts into cottages. Thus in the West, the evolution and refinement of forms in furniture, silver, ceramics, glass and other requirements for gracious living which to this day have remained basic to interior decoration did not get underway until the seventeenth century, and it was only the following century that saw their true blossoming.

Within these basic categories, and a potpourri of others relating to past domestic life, there is an enormously wide range of collecting possibilities from which to choose. In the following two chapters we will provide a brief survey of some of the categories of antiques and collectibles that are available today.

Approaches to Collecting

There are two basic approaches to collecting, each having many possible variations, and each having its advantages.

The first is collecting by categories. Many people collect narrowly defined categories of objects, usually small, such as souvenir spoons; glass or ceramic cup plates; powder flasks; tobacco boxes; glass paperweights; salt spoons; and so forth. If this type of collecting interests you, be assured that there are many sorts of attractive, small antiques and collectibles from which to choose. Such collections have the advantage that they can be easily displayed within a limited space. Another advantage to this type of collecting is that you can concentrate your knowledge within a single, highly specialized area.

The second basic approach to collecting is to select one or more historical periods of decorative art as a basis for collecting a variety of objects. There are a number of advantages

---

SPECIALIZED COLLECTIONS

Numerous people have made specialized collections centered around a theme or historical event of interest to them. People have, for example, collected objects relating to the life of birds, the development of the railroad, or the history of a particular locale or family. These very specialized collections can be difficult to assemble, but they are among the most satisfying.

Despite the scarcity of materials, a friend of mine has found a fascinating array of diverse items depicting black people: prints, paintings, old books, English regency bronzes, and ceramics. She has collected a variety of British ceramics related to the anti-slavery cause, especially representations of the characters from UNCLE TOM'S CABIN in Staffordshire figures and plates and on various textiles. She also has an anti-slavery lustre jug made in the early nineteenth century. In assembling this type of collection, dealers who specialize in historical materials are particularly helpful.

A rare anti-slavery jug made in Staffordshire, circa 1815–20. (Illustration 93a, "Old English Lustre Pottery" by W. D. John and Warren Baker.) On reverse side:

The Negro's Complaint

Fleecy locks and black complexion
Cannot forfeit nature's claim:
Skins may differ but affection
Dwells in white and black the same.
Slaves of gold whose sordid dealings
Tarnish all your boasted powers:
Prove that you have human feelings,
Ere you boldly question ours.

to this historical approach to collecting; different styles of decorative art, combined with care, not only settle down well together but actually seem to enhance one another's charms. This method of collecting allows for more choices, which is a great advantage in today's market.

The second approach is particularly useful if you are interested in furnishing and decorating a home. If a certain amount of furniture is basic to your plans, that is a good place to begin your collecting. For practical purposes you will find that tables of all sorts as well as case pieces, such as chests of drawers, desks, cupboards, and sideboards are usually more satisfactory than antique seating furniture, which is sometimes difficult and expensive to keep functional.

Many successful collectors have combined the historical approach with the collection of small categories. Once you have furnished your home, your collecting interests may turn to a specialty, perhaps to enhance your decor, but perhaps to provide a new outlet for your increased interest in and knowledge of antiques.

Other Considerations: Time, Money, and Space

In making basic decisions about collecting, most of us have to take into account personal limitations in time, money, and space. This book was not written for the amasser who simply wants to accumulate hoards of things with little regard to what they are, but rather for the collector who is interested in antiques because they warm his heart and embellish his life. It is your choice whether you will have a small collection of things that please you completely, or a much larger one which contains few things of which that may be said. But very few people who choose quality are dissatisfied with their decision.

When you first get started, antiques may seem to be rather expensive, luxury items, but if you choose carefully, they will give you lifelong satisfaction, and as an agreeable bonus will retain, or even increase, their market value. The same cannot be said for most of the "durable goods" that are available today. Most modern furnishings are not only aesthetically very unremarkable, but also expensive, enjoy a relatively short life, and have little if any resale value. You may be pleasantly surprised to discover, for instance, that often "old" flatware and dishes are not only more carefully made than new, but frequently more reasonably priced as well. Even in today's tight market you may find the same to be true of at least certain types and styles of antique and collectible furniture. Though you may find yourself sometimes saving money in buying old rather than new, the real bargain will be in the lasting pleasure of an object you have consciously chosen and love.

Where to Find Information

Especially when you are first starting to collect, it is best to concentrate on one area of interest. Beginning with whatever you want most, look, study, get all the information you can. This is the fastest way to learn, and when you turn to something else and repeat the process, you will be delighted to see how much more easily you learn. In selecting that first area of interest, and in learning about it, you will find the following sources for information invaluable

1) the decorative arts collections in museums

2) books

3) shops and shows

The best place to start in looking at antiques and collectibles is the decorative arts department of a museum. Here you will see objects, many of which only a few years ago were still on the market; so what you are seeing is a special sort of successful collecting. Museums try to acquire objects that embody those characteristics of a period that several generations of antiquarians and collectors have found most desirable. You should study these collections carefully to make yourself familiar with the qualities in antiques that have stood the test of time. You will not understand why there can be such a difference in price between objects that seem very much alike until you have done the looking necessary to train your eyes and to be able to sort out the differences. You will probably agree with the ideas of desirability that have been the choice of earlier collectors. In any event, you will have to take into account how important they are in today's market.

Make notes on what objects most appeal to you; these will help you to find books at the library which will give you more information and probably show more examples. Books can be a great help in surveying the field. The following books, with their historical backgrounds, accurate descriptions, and splendid illustrations, provide an excellent survey of the whole range of decorative arts in America.

Marshall B. Davidson (author and editor in charge). *The American Heritage History of Antiques* in 3 vols. 1967-69.

Elizabeth Stillinger. *The Antiques Guide to Decorative Arts in America: 1600–1875*. 1972. E. P. Dutton & Co.

Helen Comstock, *ed. The Concise Encyclopedia of American Antiques*. New York: Hawthorne Books, Inc.

If your interest is in American furniture, you will find the books by Helen Comstock, Joseph Downs, Dean Fales, John Kirk, Charles Montgomery, and Albert Sack, all listed in the bibliography at the end of this book, particularly useful; you will progress more rapidly if you make separate studies of

British and American furniture. Confusions can result if they are studied at once, but for many reasons you will need to know which is which. If silver is your interest, you will also want to study both British and American silver, again separately.

The bibliography provided in this book should be of help to you in planning surveys for whatever categories of antiques or collectibles are of interest to you. Our bibliography does not, of course, contain all the good books, but the listings are intended to include the best books currently available; many of these books contain their own extensive bibliographies.

As you continue to learn more about antiques and collectibles, books will become increasingly important to you. At the public library you can familiarize yourself with collectors' books before deciding on which you want to buy, both for your chosen area and for information on the field in general. Making use of the excellent research now available will help you greatly in overcoming some of the handicaps of today's tight market.

Once you have prepared yourself in your chosen area by careful reading and looking in museums, you will be ready to enter the market place. At first you will want simply to look, to familiarize yourself with its operations, to learn what is currently available and what the prices are. In the chapters of this book which deal with the marketplace — shops, shows, auctions, and so forth — suggestions will be made that will permit you to use them as part of your education without becoming *persona non grata* with dealers or auctioneers.

Beginning to Buy

After you have completed your research and have sufficiently familiarized yourself with the market, you will be ready to buy that first fine piece. Of course you will not always know everything there is to know about a particular item each time you buy. Today's market often requires that you be able to decide rather quickly whether or not you want a given object. But if you have provided yourself with an adequate background in your area of interest, you should have a good general idea about when, of what, and how the object you are considering was made; you should also be able to determine its quality and whether or not you wish to buy. You will have the leisure afterwards to find out more exactly what it is.

To illustrate from my own experience: once while I was still rather new to collecting, I saw a truly exquisite eighteenth century Chinese export plate. Though I was then familiar in general with the ceramics and decorative art of that period, I knew little about Chinese export ware. Nonetheless I felt that I had to have the dish. Fortunately I had the money saved and I was able to buy it. Afterwards I checked all the books I could find on the subject, and asked all the specialist dealers from here and the East coast about the plate; my inquiries revealed that I had bought a truly unusual piece. To me it is the best buy I ever made — though one of the most expensive — and it has given me endless satisfaction.

Though the plate's rarity adds to its monetary value, its real value to me lies in the aesthetic qualities for which I bought it at the time. Your best guide to buying antiques is not a search for age and rarity as such, but for the aesthetic qualities which make an object desirable regardless of when it was made. It is of course one of the facts of life that many of the most beautiful objects are now both old and rare. At one time perhaps they were not particularly rare, but the ravages of time and the desires of many earlier collectors to possess them have made them so. The Chinese export plate illustrates that objects that are beautiful, old and rare do turn up in the Midwest if you keep your eyes open and know what to look for.

The final word of advice comes from a young, midwestern collector of American glass whom I interviewed for *The National Antiques Review:*

> His advice to collectors is what he takes himself: buying and reading books is the best investment one can make to get the answers to the questions of what was made — how, where, when and by whom. Go to museums, look, and ask questions. Go to shows and *look;* whether you can afford to buy or not. When buying, try to get the best examples of the particular types, and the diversity of a well-rounded collection. Buy pieces that are as perfect as possible, being aware that the greater the rarity, the more signs of age have to be accepted. Sometimes buy above what may have seemed to be the going price — in these days of growing scarcity and vanishing rarities it is often difficult to say what is the "right price" — and the "rare one" gets away and the opportunity may not come again.[1]

An ethereal, hexagonal eighteenth century brass and glass lantern, probably French. Happily it has a delicious patina; polishing the brass parts of such a delicate object, without damage, would be difficult. Bought from dealer for $65; valued at $300.

2

Special Conditions
in the Midwest Antiques Market

Only a few generations ago the Midwest was a vast territory of wilderness and prairie with a few frontier outposts. In contrast, the eastern beachheads which became the thirteen colonies, and which in this century produced the eastern antiques market, enjoyed about 200 years of development before they felt the great changes brought about by the industrial revolution. The economic and cultural progress which took place in the colonies and in the early years of the republic made possible the development of an indigenous architecture and decorative arts which, especially in furniture and silver, comprise our most important heritage of antiques.

The settlement and development of the Midwest was very different. The eastern pioneers who came to their new home-sites in the Midwest were severely limited in the number as well as the size of the household possessions they could bring with them in overland travel; the bulk of their possessions, especially the larger pieces, had to be left in the East.

By the mid-nineteenth century economic progress in much of the Midwest permitted the spartanism of the frontier to be gradually replaced with a more "luxurious" way of life.

Technological developments in the making of furniture, metals, ceramics, and glass ensured the ability of thriving new manufacturers to provide the necessities of life for an increasingly comfortable home. Industrialization hastened the decline of handcraftsmanship, but it has provided us today with a large number of 100-year-old machine-made "antiques". The changes wrought by technology, however, did not come everywhere at the same time. For many years country furniture was made by traditional methods and in traditional styles in many parts of the territory. This late country furniture of the frontier has always existed in the Midwest and is bought and sold here today. Handcraftsmanship lingered on in the Midwest in other crafts as well, such as in silver and other metalworking.

Because the Midwest was settled later than the eastern United States, the objects that interest the collector of the eighteenth and early nineeenth century periods have gener-

Stage coach trunk, wood-covered with animal skin (deer or steer) with the hair left on. The hardware is original except for the hinges, and the original wallpaper lining is intact. Late eighteenth or early nineteenth century. Bought at auction for $5; valued at $200.

ally come to us by an entirely different route. For the most part, these earlier antiques were brought into the Midwest only after Midwesterners became consciously interested in collecting. Because there was little general interest in antiques before World War I, it was not until after 1920 that any appreciable number of them were available. From then on dealers began to operate in large cities; particularly in the earlier years they brought in large quantities of English and French antiques, which were then of greater interest here than American antiques. There were a few Midwestern dealers and collectors of American antiques, but at first their buying and selling was mainly confined to the eastern United States. For collectors of many sorts of early Americana the pattern remains much the same today. However, the American antiques of the eastern United States are becoming badly depleted, and lately there has been a steady trickle of American as well as English and French antiques from the Midwest back to the eastern states, and even back to England and France.

In the large Midwestern cities boatloads of early European antiques have continued to arrive at a steady pace from the 1920s to the present, with the greatest increase starting in the 1940s. If there has been a consistent trend in Midwestern collecting from the 1920s to today, it is that English antiques have been by far the most popular, followed by French and American antiques. Of course today French antiques are very scarce, and there is a greatly increased interest in Americana here as well as in other parts of the country.

In the Midwest, unlike the East, museums have generally had less influence on collecting tastes than the architects and interior designers who worked in the cities from the 1920s to the beginning of the 1950s. Those suburban palaces built by the very rich created an interest in antiques and fortunately have provided us with local sources now that many of these huge houses are being abandoned by their original owners for smaller quarters. This circumstance continues to enrich museums as well as private collectors. Increasing numbers of dealers and collectors are now sorting out these antiques as they emerge from large city estate sales.

Because so many antiques which were brought into the Midwest earlier are now finding their way back to the market place, and because many indigenous antiques and collectibles are still available, the Midwest offers much more to the collector than most people realize. Moreover, purchases here can often be very advantageous. Our public has had fewer opportunities to review and study excellent collections of decorative art than has been the case in the East. Although much has been and is being done here by collectors' groups to bring about a better understanding of our heritage in the decorative arts, it is nonetheless true that knowledge has not kept up with the opportunities offered here. For all these reasons, the Midwest has been called, quite correctly I believe, a buyer's market.

My own experience and that of friends and acquaintances is that even in today's tight market place, opportunities often turn up to buy excellent pieces priced well below the current market.

The objects illustrated in this chapter were all bought by collectors with a general interest in antiques of the eighteenth or early nineteenth centuries rather than in very specific objects from a narrowly defined category. These people are too sensible to be bargain hunters; rather, they simply buy the best antiques in their area of interest that they can find and afford. But when they find such objects offered at low prices by dealers, or at auctions where they attract little interest and bidding, they are of course delighted to have their knowledge pay off.

In the following chapters, which survey the broad range of collectibles and antiques, we will provide further illustrations of good buys that have been made in the Midwest. The

Plain high-style American Chippendale, tilt-top table, an urn column supported by a reverse curve tripod base with snake feet. The grain of the wood of the top is well handled; the patina a glorious amber. Circa 1770-80. Bought at an auction where British and Continental imports were being sold. It seems probable that this table made a round trip to Britain — was it a fleeing Tory or someone else at a later time? Sold for $120; appraised for $4,500.

examples given in this book are for the most part early antiques, which are rarer and more difficult to find than later pieces. They were chosen to show that by knowing about such objects, you not only may find them in the Midwest, but can occasionally buy them for considerably less than their usual prices. The objects presented in this book were all bought and appraised in the Midwest within the last four years. All prices paid are retail prices, and the transactions were made without haggling.

It is important to note, however, that antiques (and their prices) are not easily comparable. It is meaningless to discuss price without reference to the age of an object, its aesthetic qualities and condition, its historical associations and many other factors, including just where and when it was most recently purchased. For this reason even the best price guides are of little use in most categories except in giving compara tive prices.

If you examine the price guide listed in our bibliography, you can get a very good idea of how prices for Anglo-American historical china compare in general with the prices for Carnival glass. But you cannot use any price guide to determine exactly what you should pay for a particular item in any category. You cannot, for example, determine how much you should pay for a slant-top desk on the basis of a price guide. The price for such a desk could vary from $150 to $15,000 or more. If, for example, you wanted to buy one of the better Rhode Island block front desks, you would need to have more than $65,000 in your checking account. The price would depend on a whole host of variables such as those mentioned above. Your surest guide to current prices is simply to go into the market place, to shops and shows, and examine as many examples of the items that interest you as you can. See what they are selling for and take into account their quality and condition.

One of a pair of silver salt dishes made by Wood & Hughes, New York, N.Y., circa 1845. Rope applied to edges — loop and tassel handles — gilded interiors. Bought at an elegant shop for $95; valued at $500.

What will be clear from reading the guide listed in our bibliography is that it is unwise to decide that older pieces must be ruled out of your plans because of price. Many collectibles made in this century are very expensive because they are fashionable. Before you decide what you can afford or cannot afford, go into the market place and do some comparative pricing. And remember that the most important consideration in the purchase of any antique or collectible is the authentic, excellent object, whether it is priced above or below what is currently considered the "market price".

We in the Midwest are indebted to earlier collectors and dealers for the excellent taste reflected in the objects they were responsible for bringing into and keeping in this area. To a large degree their interest in fine objects from the past is what has made the Midwest such a good place to buy.

**Caughley soft-paste porcelain coffee pot, blue printed in "Birds
in Tree" design. Caughley coffee pots are quite rare; this one
is marked with an S — circa 1775–85. Bought from dealer for
$185; valued at $425.**

3

Survey of the Field: **ANTIQUES**

This survey of "antiques" and, in the next chapter, "collect-ibles", is intended to give you an overview of the great diversity of objects from the past which you might want to collect. Our survey is limited for the most part to those objects that have been used by Americans, as these are more widely available. Some of these objects were made here; others were made elsewhere and imported for the American market, sometimes in large quantities. This survey is necessarily fragmentary, and the topics are chosen somewhat arbitrarily, for it would be impossible to describe in a brief chapter or two the enormous diversity of available objects; the bibliography provides a wealth of material which should help you to round out our survey as well as to study in much more depth categories that may be of special interest to you.

If we go back to America's origins, we see a vast, sparsely inhabited continent with no easily exploited wealth such as gold or silver; the earliest period of American history permitted little beyond mere survival and produced almost nothing for the antique collector. Yet, within a century, the settlers had successfully transplanted within this wilderness a European culture subtly shaped by colonial experience into a distinctively American style.

The eighteenth century was the golden age of decorative arts in the West, and one in which the colonialists participated fully. Life then had fewer distractions; life centered on the home and on making it as comfortable and attractive as possible. In Europe a knowledge of the decorative arts was considered part of the education of a gentleman, who as a result took an active role in the design of his house, furniture and other appointments. These were then made largely on special order by craftsmen who were highly skilled from long years of training in the carefully regulated guild system. Their skill and the taste of their wealthy clientele combined to produce the many magnificent objects we admire today.

The colonists brought with them, though in somewhat transmuted forms, the same skills and traditions that had made European decorative arts of this period so fine. Although there was never a guild system in colonial America, the maintenance of the apprentice system in the more populous towns assured high standards of craftsmanship, and given the shortage of skilled labor, craftsmen were particularly esteemed and influential members of colonial society. As in Europe, those who could afford to, took a keen interest in their houses and furnishings, and wealthier Americans eagerly followed the latest fashions from abroad; though direct design influences were for the most part English, Americans were also quite interested in the Chinese and French styles which were the predominant influences then in European taste.

Life in the colonies, however, was different than in Europe. The hardships of early settlement as well as the constant presence of the frontier encouraged a versatile, self-reliant population interested in a balance of function and ornament.

42

The difficulties of transportation and communications as well as the influence of varied ethnic groups, such as the Dutch in New York and the Germans in Pennsylvania, encouraged the development of diverse regional styles.

Even the wealthiest Americans had to work for their incomes, and as a result had more practical interests and were more modest in their style of life. The great American houses were smaller and their furnishings, which were on a correspondingly smaller scale, had a directness of proportions and a simplicity of ornamentation which distinguished American taste from European.

Western traditions of craftsmanship, as well as the taste which supported them, continued in many crafts well into the nineteenth century both in Europe and in the early American republic; this is fortunate, inasmuch as objects from the nineteenth century exist in much greater abundance than those of earlier centuries, and are more reasonably priced.

FURNITURE

The category of decorative art most basic to domestic life was and is furniture. As the term is used in the antiques trade, "furniture" refers not only to chairs, beds, tables, chests and other objects that we usually think of as furniture, but also to other related items, usually constructed primarily of wood, such as clocks, barometers, mirrors, writing and sewing boxes, spice cabinets, and so forth.

American Furniture — At one time American furniture was seen simply as a plainer and lesser version of English furniture, but it is now recognized that American cabinetmakers used the English styles of William and Mary, Queen Anne, Chippendale, Helpplewhite, and Sheraton to create a distinctively American furniture of unquestioned excellence. Because the population of the colonies and early republic was so much smaller and its wealth so much more modest than that of Great Britain and the Continent, American furniture, especially in its earlier and choicer forms, is not abundant. This relative scarcity of American furniture, along with the current recognition of its great desirability, have made the better examples of American cabinet making quite expensive.

Nonetheless, there still is much to choose from in the wide and interesting diversity of furniture which was made during our early history, first as a colony, then as a nation. These include the high style, formal furniture of the major urban centers, such as Boston, Newport, Philadelphia, New York and Baltimore, each of which developed its own regional characteristics.

"Country" furniture, which shows equally pronounced regional characteristics, ranges from the rather elegant but simplified versions of high style furniture made in many smaller but still prosperous towns to primitive pieces made by farmers for their own use, or by a jack-of-all-tradesman on the frontier. Country furniture includes the justly famous American Windsor chair, though such chairs were used as much in the city as in the country; it also includes that triumph of early mass production, the Hitchcock fancy chair, and other delights such as Salem rockers.

Plain and fancy painted furniture is an important subcategory of American furniture, and now in particular it is considered highly desirable. Almost from the beginning paint was used on American furniture, either to protect the wood or to decorate it. Most country furniture, including the Windsor and the Hitchcock chair just mentioned, was originally painted, as was some high style furniture. Now that the value of all old finishes, including paint, is more generally recognized, furniture which retains its old paint has become much more sought after than examples which have been stripped.

44

New England windsor chair, a fine example from the top of the curve of its bowed back rail to the bold rake of its legs; this handsome chair retains mellowed red paint. Circa 1800–20.

In formal furniture a variety of decorative painting was used. In the early and mid-eighteenth century, such furniture was sometimes japanned, a technique which used varnish, paint and gilding, in imitation of the Oriental lacquers then popular. Later, gilding and other decorative painting was used on Federal, fancy, and Empire furniture. Decorative painting and stencilling (stencils were called theorems then) were taught to many respectable young ladies in the "female schools" that flourished in the early nineteenth century; this type of decoration can be found on such objects as small sewing tables and boxes. Clocks and looking glasses also were often decorated with paint.

Country furniture was most often "plain painted", that is, painted in a single color, but frequently it was quite fanci-

45

fully decorated, with the designs sometimes a freewheeling imitation of the more elaborate woods and decoration used on formal furniture. Yet another and more idiosyncratic type of painting is found on the furniture classified as American folk art.

Country furniture, whether painted or not, is available in a great variety of styles and types in the Midwest, as there are many good dealers here who make it their specialty. Inevitably, later styles are more abundant than earlier ones. City furniture of the eighteenth century is seldom for sale here, but if this is what you want, keep an eye out for it. It does sometimes turn up.

Shaker furniture can be classified as a part of American country furniture. Nonetheless, in terms of style and craftsmanship, Shaker products differ from the main trend of American furniture because of the separate and distinctive life-style of the Shakers. This remarkable religious communal sect — the United Society of Believers in Christ's Second Appearing, as they called themselves — came to America from England in the late eighteenth century. For many generations it went its well-organized, industrious, and peaceful way in, but not of, a country quickly becoming more complicated and worldly. At a time when the outside world was plunging ever farther into the excesses of Victorian design, the Shakers continued to adhere to a chaste, functional simplicity which fits well with our own modern tastes. As a result, Shaker-crafted articles of all sorts are very fashionable today, and consequently very expensive. If you wish to buy Shaker objects, first learn to recognize the proportions and methods of craftsmanship unique to their products. Many reproductions of Shaker furniture and crafts are available, most of them produced with no intention to deceive. If you are interested in Shaker reproductions, choose carefully, because there is a considerable variance in quality.

Victorian furniture is of great interest to many people native to the Midwest. This was often the first elegant furniture

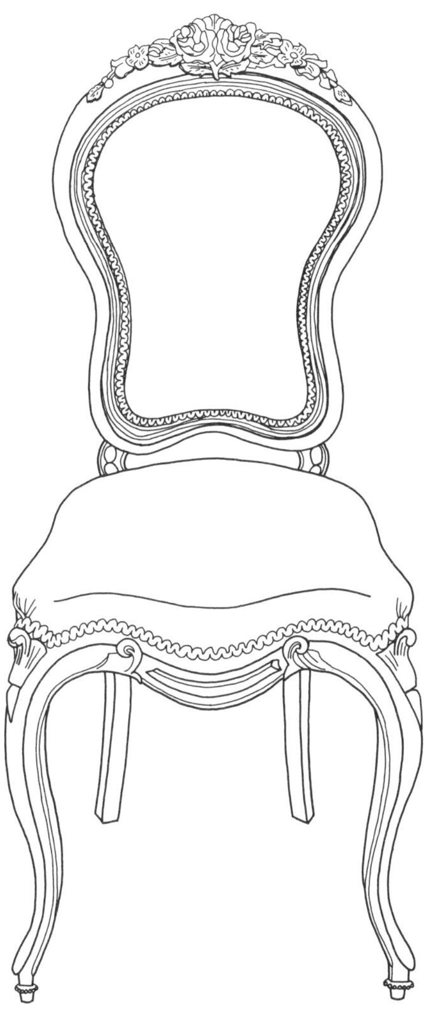

American Victorian rosewood Louis XV revival chair, circa 1850–60. The "revivals" were quite different from the revived styles; chairs such as this had a style and charm of their own. This one has an agreeable shape, splendid carving — and it is most comfortable.

bought by the ancestors of the people living here now, and so it has an heirloom feeling about it. This furniture will be described in more detail in the following chapter on collectibles. Victorian furniture of the pre-1875 period shares with the later furniture many of the same characteristics: in particular, an increasing eclecticism in sources for design unrestrained by traditional methods of craftsmanship, increasingly massive proportions, and elaborate ornamentation. Nonetheless, some of the best Victorian designs, especially those made in the French rococo revival style were made in this period. Victorian design varies in quality and is not always the best, but much of the furniture made is attractive as well as sturdy and comfortable. The quality of the woods used and the workmanship is generally quite high. Victorian furniture is abundant in the Midwest, and some of it is still quite inexpensive.

British Furniture — A wide variety of British furniture of the eighteenth and early nineteenth centuries is available in the Midwest, ranging from elegant pieces made for city or large country houses to simple cottage-type furniture. Although it is much less costly than its American counterpart, it can still be quite expensive. Generally speaking, British furniture is aesthetically pleasing and soundly made, often from very fine and attractive woods. You will find that the Midwest is an excellent place to find this furniture, whatever your particular preferences are.

Although there are many similarities between British and American furniture, it is useful to become aware of certain characteristic differences. British furniture is often more elaborate in its design and use of woods than American furniture. In particular, veneering appears more frequently on British furniture, and some of these richly grained veneers are quite different from those used in American cabinetmaking. British veneered case pieces, such as desks and chests, can be quite

English mahogany four-drawer chest, with slide, made in second half of eighteenth century. The drawers are lipped and the pierced brasses are elegant and old. This small, excellently proportioned, very desirable chest has bracket feet. Such chests are easily found in the Midwest.

elegant and lovely. They can do much to dress up an interior, and they often combine very well with American or French furniture.

The British made a much greater variety of furniture forms than did the Americans, and many of their smaller pieces, such as small tables, candlestands, and cellarettes, are attractive and useful in the modern home. Most of the mirrors and barometers on the market today are British in origin; the British also made a much wider variety of trays and small boxes than were ever made in America. Understandably, even the most avid collectors of Americana sometimes cannot resist the charms of these smaller pieces.

ANTIQUES WITH MOVING PARTS

If clocks, watches and music boxes are sold in running order, ask if there is a warranty, and if so, for what length of time, and how it will be implemented. This information should be part of your receipt.

Do not expect a warranty for barometers. It is difficult to keep them operational, and in any case they are usually bought primarily for their decorative qualities. The same is true of automata. If they operate when bought, that is all you can usually expect.

Clocks and Watches

Music Boxes

Barometers

Automata: dolls, animals, birds, human figures

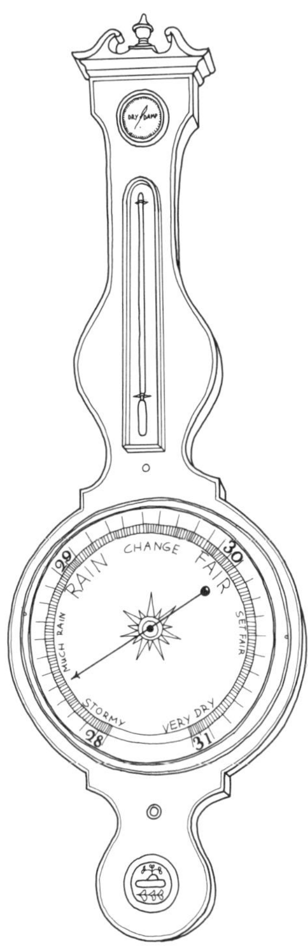

"P & P Gally 9 Turnmill Str.ᵗ Clerkenwell London" is engraved on the brass face of this excellently proportioned wheel barometer. Mahogany case with dark and light stringing and amber patina. Early nineteenth century. Bought at a house sale for $125 — four years later appraised for $750.

French Furniture — Formal French furniture includes some of the finest examples of cabinetmaking in the Western world. Its excellence was recognized by collectors from the beginning, and as a result it is now very scarce and enormously costly. However, such furniture is found here occasionally, so if this is what you want, be prepared to recognize the genuine piece if and when you find it.

French provincial furniture, a simplified or "country" version of French formal or high style furniture, is much more available and quite attractive. Provincial furniture is usually made in solid woods such as walnut, beech and wild cherry, or has simple veneers in these woods as opposed to the elaborate veneers, marketry, gilding and other embellishments characteristic of formal French furniture.

French provincial writing table (bureau plat) in walnut which is much lighter in color than American walnut. A simple table of superb proportions and graceful lines. No pulls on drawers. Leather top. Circa 1770.

SILVER

Historically, silver has been referred to in a variety of ways, and it may be of some use to define a few basic terms before proceeding. Our ancestors spoke of all silver, both hollow-ware and flatware, as "plate". This term, which still appears in some books, should not be confused with the modern term "plate", meaning electroplated silver: that is, a base metal with a thin coating of pure silver. Our ancestors' "plate" was usually either sterling or coin silver. Both sterling and coin are alloys of silver. Sterling is 925/1000 parts fine, which means 925 parts silver to 75 parts alloy, all or most of which is copper. Coin silver is 900/1000, or nine parts silver to one

Silver tea caddy made by Hall & Hewson & Co. working in Albany, N.Y., circa 1820. On opposite side is engraved "Green Tea" and "PCL". Tea caddies are rare in American silver. Pieces with Baltimore assay marks are also rare.

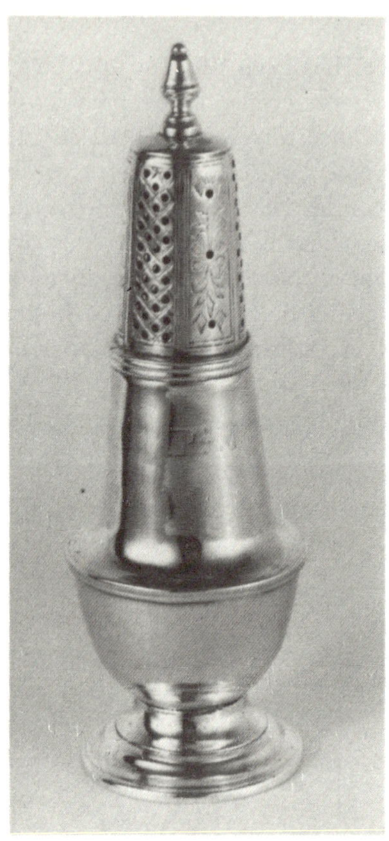

Silver caster by Samuel Minott (1732–1803), Boston, circa 1770. Vase shaped on splayed foot, pierced and engraved cover in six panels, bell form finial. Engraved P ✝ M to right of seam. Despite two brothers who were captains in the Concord militia, Samuel Minott was not a sterling patriot. He was marked for his Tory views when he sided with the royal appointee, Gov. Hutchinson, in 1774. An excellent silversmith, starting his career in 1758 making tutorial plate, he was still working in Boston in 1796.

part alloy. Occasionally the silver content of an object is greater or lesser, and is usually marked as such. The color of silver is unaffected by changes in the amount of alloy unless the silver content is reduced to less than 800/1000. Some alloy is necessary in any silver object inasmuch as silver made up without alloy is too soft to be practical.

As with furniture, the foundation for silver making in America as well as in Britain and on the Continent was the apprentice system. Because of the crucial role of the silversmith in handling monetary assets (silver objects were made in large measure from surplus boullion, and could always be converted to boullion again), the system was strictly regulated, and with splendid results.

American Silver — Martha Gandy Fales states in her invaluable guide to the subject, *Early American Silver,* that "silver represents the first important art form in this country. The historical events with which silver objects are associated rep-

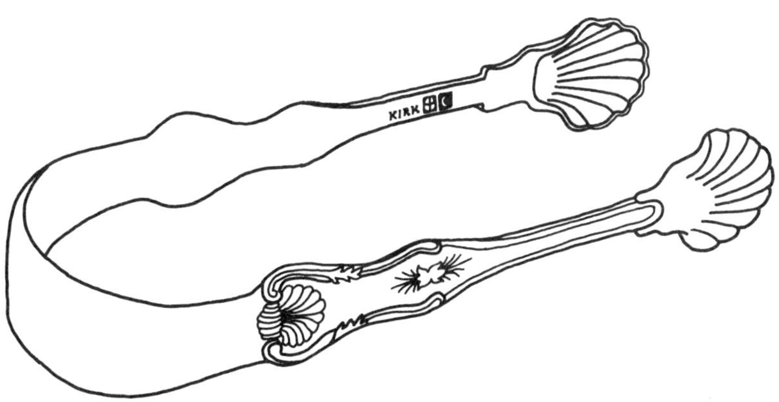

Silver sugar tongs by William Kirk having the Baltimore assay mark for 1827. Kings pattern with shell grips.

resent major aspects of our development as a nation . . . Silver makes history come alive. But more than that it represents one of our country's greatest cultural legacies."[2]

From the beginning, silvermaking played an extraordinarily important role in the American colonies. Because there were no banks or safe deposit boxes, Americans put their hard-earned savings largely into silver objects. The need for the silversmith as a substitute banker explains why the craft was so widespread in the colonies and why, given the small size of the populace and its rather modest wealth as compared to Europe, such an abundance of silver was made. Of course much silver was lost in the Revolutionary War, whether it was taken by fleeing Tory sympathizers or the invading British, or was melted down by American patriots to finance the war. And, as was true everywhere, much silver was melted down simply to be refashioned in newer styles. In the United States a famous example of the latter was Mrs. Grover Cleveland's decision to have the official White House silver, which had been made during the Madison administration, melted down so it could be refashioned into flatware more useful for turn-of-the-century entertaining at the White House.

Because early American silver is now rare and expensive, it is difficult to collect, but its restrained perfection and historical significance make it well worth the effort. Even a few small pieces can give you great satisfaction. I have made some remarkable buys in the Midwest even though it is especially scarce here. You should study American silver well before you buy it because it requires know-how to collect, even if your funds are unlimited. Moreover, you will enjoy it more fully if you understand its historical background.

British Silver—Antique British silver, which so clearly demonstrates the remarkable expertise fostered by the guild system, is quite desirable for collecting. Britain was a great imperial power when most of its silver was made, as is evident in the

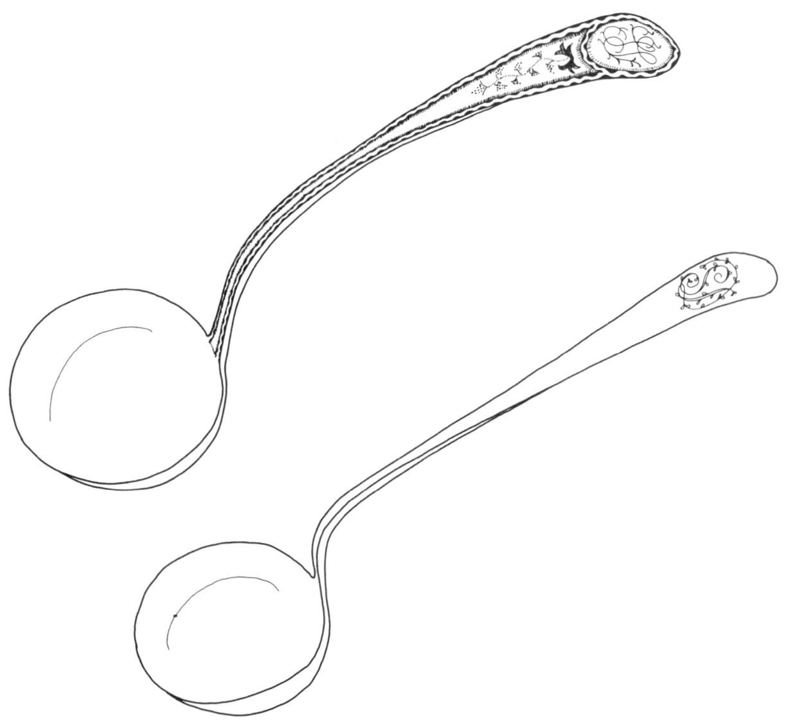

Two eighteenth century Philadelphia silver punch ladles:

above, back bent handle with slightly pointed end, bright cut edges and foliate monogramming in cartouche. Made by John Myers, apprentice of Richard Humphries (who made silver for George Washington; the latter was an apprentice of Philip Syng), circa 1785. Myers made the tray presented by the Board of Managers of Philadelphia Hospitals to Dr. Benjamin Rush for his services during the yellow fever epidemic of 1798.

below, old English pattern ladle with backward bent, round bowl and foliate initials by William Taylor, circa 1775–80.

George II silver milk jug by Benjamin Sanders, London 1743. Pear-shaped body with cast cabriole legs and cast double-scroll handle. Serrated rim and short drawn pouring lip. Except that a longer applied lip was much used, this jug is very similar to American milk pots made in this style. Bought for $250. American milk pots are much more expensive.

enormous amounts that were produced as well as in its quality. There is still much from which to choose, making it a pleasure to collect. Another advantage to the collector is that it is very well marked; British silver has had a stable system of hallmarks since Renaissance times, well before the eighteenth and nineteenth centuries, which provide most of the silver on the market today. This system of hallmarks makes it possible for you to know where, when, and often by whom a given piece was made. See the bibliography for books which can assist you in identifying hallmarks. British silver is ex-

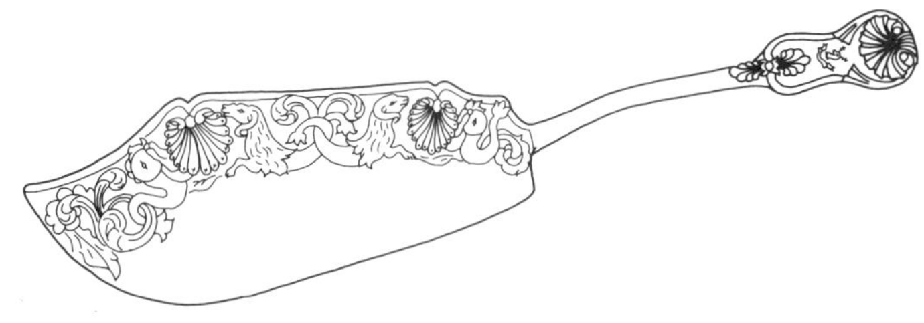

Silver fish slice by Robert Gray & Son, Glásgow 1839. Engraved with sea horses, shells, etc. — crested.

pensive but well worth the price, and the Midwest is a good place to buy it.

French Silver — French silver is, to quote John Marshall Graham II in his introduction to the catalog of the Campbell Museum, "the rarest of all silver . . . as so much went to the melting pots to defray the cost of wars. France produced in silver the most beautiful and sophisticated designs that the world has known."[3] Its rarity and cost make it almost impossible to collect in its most desirable forms. Nonetheless, the study of French silver is useful, for here you will see the origins of many types of silver with which we are familiar either indirectly, because of the Huguenot influence on British silver, or directly, because of the many Huguenot silversmiths who settled in America.

Sheffield Plate — In the mid-eighteenth century a group of English craftsmen developed a less costly method for producing silver articles by fusing silver to copper, and then working the sheets into objects. A variety of objects, often of excellent design and workmanship, were made for about 100 years, after which Sheffield plate was superceded by the easier and less expensive method of electroplating. Sheffield plate is quite desirable to collect, but before you start consult the appropiate books, and then seek out a knowlegeable dealer.

HALLMARKS

A hallmark is a set of symbols stamped on an object made of silver or gold. The British system of hallmarks dates from the fourteenth century and is still in operation. It has four elements:

The **STANDARD MARK** indicates that the piece meets one of the various minimum standards for gold or silver content.

The **ASSAY OFFICE MARK** identifies the town in which the gold or silver was tested by the government.

The **DATE LETTER** verifies the date the piece was made.

The **MAKER'S MARK** identifies the goldsmith or silversmith who produced the piece. The terms Goldsmith and Silversmith are virtually interchangeable because these craftsmen were trained to work in both metals. Goldsmith is the older term.

Nations other than Britain also had their own systems of hallmarks, and the collector of their silver and gold objects will need to learn them.

The markings on American silver are not called hallmarks because they do not reflect a uniform and consistent system. This lack of systematic markings makes American silver much harder to identify than English silver.

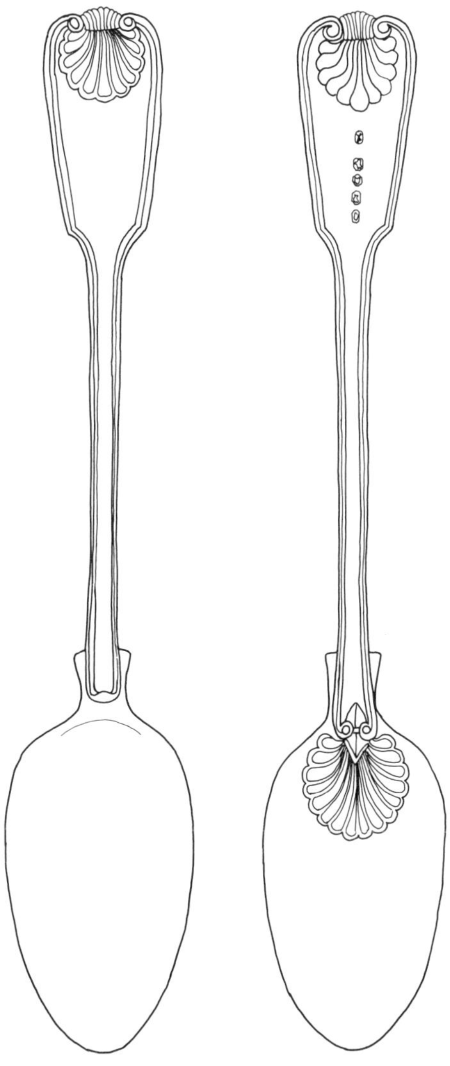

Front and back of silver stuffing spoon by George Angel, London 1854. Fiddle thread and shell — crested. Paid $60; valued at $150. Note hallmarks on the back of the spoon's handle.

CERAMICS

Ceramics comprise the largest and richest of the major categories in antiques. From ancient times, earthen pots and dishes have been an essential part of domestic life, and since the necessary clay is easy to find, pottery-making has been almost universal. Though initially pottery was made simply to meet daily needs for food preparation and storage and for eating and drinking, in most places it also developed into an art form, as archeological finds attest.

As navigation improved and trade with the far East was established, the imported custom of tea-drinking provided a new impetus to the development of ceramics. The China trade had an important influence on the whole of Western decorative art, but nowhere was this influence felt more strongly than in ceramics. In the seventeenth and eighteenth centuries, the new taste on the Continent and in England and Colonial America for elegant living led to a great vogue for Oriental wares, though few people except the very wealthy could afford to buy the furniture, hand-painted wallpaper, silk, lacquer, and porcelain made in China for the Western trade. But the drinking of tea, as costly as it then was, became the aspiration of the many, as well as the height of fashion for the few. Thus tea drinking, and soon afterward, the drinking of coffee and chocolate, provided the impetus, long lacking in the West, for the making of ceramics which would be both more useful and more elegant.

When tea from China was first imported by Western traders, the porcelain tea bowls also had to be imported, since there were no suitable vessels made domestically for drinking tea. For centuries in the West, ale, cider, and wine were the beverages drunk by those who could afford them at breakfast as well as throughout the day; none of the vessels used for these beverages was appropriate for tea. Ale and cider were drunk, as one descended in the social scale, from silver tankards, pewter mugs, wooden mugs called "noggins", or leather mugs called "black jacks". Wine drinkers used similar vessels unless they were among the lucky few who could afford glass (for domestic purposes glassware was not generally available until the eighteenth century). Chinese porce-

A group of first period Worchester soft-paste porcelain, left to right: milk jug transfer printed in blue, blue painted open crescent mark; basket with transfer printed "Pine Cone" design in blue in center, reticulated rim hand painted on inside, with painted florets on outside; small sauce boat hand painted in blue in chinoiserie design on one side, flowers on other side, inside, lip and handle blue painted, open crescent mark (see G. A. Godden: Caughley and Worchester Porcelains 1775–1800 #293, Praeger, N.Y.); cup and saucer transfer printed in floral pattern shown on page 44 of above Godden book.
Photograph by Noel Kopald

lain was ideal for tea drinking, but in the West the only pottery available was rough, porous, and fragile. Although silver could be used for teapots, silver teacups were impractical: the cups would be too hot to handle, and so much metal ruined the delicate flavors and aromas of the teas. For several generations we have been surrounded by so much porcelain and other ceramics that it is difficult for us to realize that until quite recently our part of the world lacked these refinements.

BASIC CERAMIC TERMS

The terms used to classify and describe ceramic objects are bewildering to the beginner because they are many, and often imprecise in their application. Here are a few essential ones.

BODY — A term which refers to the clays out of which the various types of ceramics are made. An exception is porcelain, the substance of which should always be called "paste".

GLAZE — The material applied to the body which vitrifies (becomes glass-like) when fired.

SLIP — Clay thinned to the consistency of cream and applied in designs for the purpose of decoration.

HARD PASTE PORCELAIN — A type of porcelain, produced by the Chinese for the last 2,000 years, made from kaolin and petunse. It is very vitrious, white, usually translucent, very hard. In general, only one very high temperature firing is needed to create the finished and glazed object.

Having been introduced to the pleasures of Chinese porcelain, the West determined to make porcelain for itself. The royal heads of Europe addressed themselves to the problem with much the same determination and lack of international cooperation that later characterized the discovery of the atomic bomb. The breakthrough came, after more than two generations of effort, at the end of the first decade of the eighteenth century when (using the work of von Tschirnhaus) Johann Friedrich Böttger, who worked under the patronage

---

SOFT PASTE PORCELAIN — A broad term which refers to various wares made by European potteries (beginning in the seventeenth century) in imitation of the Chinese hard paste porcelain. Ground glass and white clay are the main ingredients. It can be marked with a file, and when chipped, the body looks granular. It is fired in an unglazed state, and then glazed in subsequent lower temperature firings.

BONE CHINA — A porcelain made from a paste perfected by the first Josiah Spode, containing bone ash (thus the name). In terms of its qualities, it falls midway between hard and soft paste porcelains. Most fine porcelains made in the West still use a similar formula.

EARTHENWARE — A general term for ceramic objects made from any number of kinds and colors of bodies. It is always opaque, porous when unglazed, and fired at much lower temperatures than porcelain.

STONEWARE — A type of earthenware made with clays that vitrify at high firing temperatures. It is stronger than earthenware and non-porous even when unglazed. Jasper and basalt are two famous stonewares.

of the King of Poland, perfected a formula at Meissen for a Chinese-type, hard-paste porcelain.

During the Seven Years War the Meissen factory was sacked repeatedly at the behest of Frederick the Great, who had the best workers transferred to Berlin so that he could set up his own porcelain works there. The Seven Years War ended the best period of the great Meissen enterprise early in the third quarter of the eighteenth century. But in the meantime the hard paste formula that was developed there had spread to several of the German states and Austria. Hard paste formulas were developed independently in France about half a century after the German breakthrough, and not too long thereafter in England.

French Ceramics — During the European search for the hard paste formula, several soft pastes having a porcelain-like translucency and beauty were developed. The formulas varied among factories, and even changed within a single factory as experimentation continued. French porcelain of the soft paste variety is considered by many to be the most beautiful ceramic ever made in the West. Although more fragile than some of the other soft-paste porcelains, it has the aesthetic qualities that are so evident in French furniture, silver, and other luxury objects, and which made France the most important Western influence during this period of great creativity in the decorative arts. This porcelain can be admired in many museums, but is very difficult and costly to collect.

There are, however, two French ceramics which are available to the collector. The first are the "Vieux Paris" porcelains, the hard-paste French porcelains made by a number of factories in Paris from about 1770 to 1850. These Parisian factories were able to encroach on the exclusive privileges originally granted by the French kings to Vincennes-Sevres porcelain: namely, the right to make ornamental as well as tableware, the use of a full range of colors (not just blue and white), and gilding. The Vieux Paris porcelains were not always marked (for many of these encroachments on the privileges of Sevres were not legal), but the style is clearly French. Most of the Vieux Paris porcelains now available are classical in style and heavily gilded.

The second type of French ceramic available to collectors is a fine earthenware first made in the late eighteenth century at Creil (pronounced Cray as in *cray*on). The factory at Creil hoped to compete successfully with the British for the mass market, but found it difficult even to survive, and in the early nineteenth century Creil merged with other factories making the same type of ware, all of which is usually referred to as

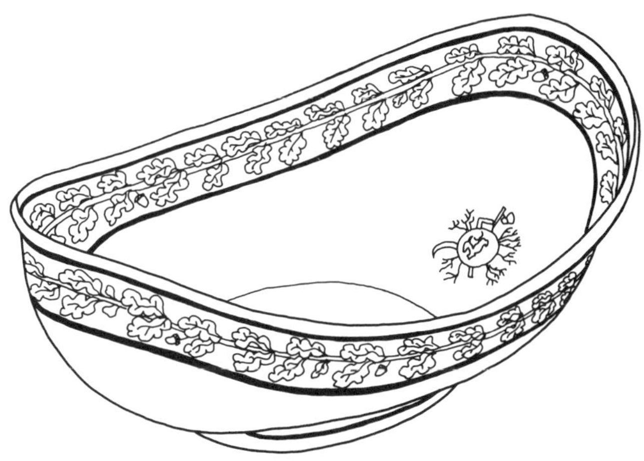

Creil: French, boat-shaped bowl of "faience fine", similar to English cream colored earthenware. Transfer printed in greenish black oak leaf banding outside and inside; a center medallion "Sylla veut incendier Rome" with cartouches on either side. Creil impressed on bottom. 12¾" long, 8¼" wide, 3¼" deep. Valued at $100.

Creil. As a result of these mergers, the marks on Creil vary, but the ware is so distinctive that it is easy to identify. Much of Creil has transfer-printed decorations, but in styles very different from those of the British. These attractive, uniquely French wares can be found in the Midwest, as can an occasional piece of French faience, a tin-glazed earthenware with hand-painted decoration.

A small reticulated earthenware basket, rope molding, scalloped top edge, twig handles, grayed lavender blue glaze and molded twisting vines and grapes in purple lustre around the handles. A lovely rarity, circa 1810. Bought from dealer for $65; valued at $425.

British Ceramics — Because the industrial revolution developed earlier in Britain than on the Continent, the British potters had no royal patronage in their early attempts to work out the many problems involved in producing on a large scale the useful and decorative wares demanded by the new and rapidly expanding interest in genteel living.

Their wares had to succeed in the market place from the beginning. As a result, the British were from the start great experimenters, and they produced for a wider market than the Continental potters. Thanks to them, we have splendid ceramics in an amazing variety of pastes, bodies, styles, and types of decoration. To name just a few, there are soft-paste porcelains, salt-glaze wares, creamware, stonewares of many sorts, including jasper and basalts, hard-paste procelains, and — to mention just one of the famous Josiah Spode's many contributions — bone china, a porcelain less hard than hard-paste but harder than soft-paste porcelain. This formula is so satisfactory that it remains a standard of fine china after nearly 200 years. The British potters' innovations in decoration were remarkable. They were the first to use transfer-printing. This technique, like many other British innovations, made it possible to produce economically, on a mass basis, aesthetically pleasing quality decoration. The British used transfer-printing in all sorts of ways, both over and under the glaze as well as in combination with other decorative techniques. Lustre, another creative British response to the need for inexpensive, attractively decorated wares, had its best period from 1805 to 1835. (See Chapter VIII for a description of this delightful ceramic.) Worcester, Caughly, Leeds, Wedgwood, Spode, Derby, and Minton are just a few of the famous British wares that can be found in the Midwest.

American Ceramics — In comparison with the Europeans, the American settlers made relatively little pottery aside from simple earthenwares and a few stonewares; these were used, along with wood, to meet everyday needs of the kitchen and table. A comparison of the ceramic shards (all that remain of this early pottery), indicates that the simple practical forms changed little over an extended period. Most of the antique American pottery collected today consists of simple earthenwares and stonewares which continued to be made well into the nineteenth century. It is usually pottery from this later period which is on the market.

For the better part of their history Americans have relied on the export trade for their "best" ceramics. There were a number of colonial efforts to produce finer ceramics, but it was impossible to compete with the mother country, which controlled the mass market in ceramics not only throughout the colonial period, but for a long time thereafter. Mass production of ceramics required a large capital investment, and

---

DECORATIVE TECHNIQUES APPLIED TO CERAMICS

SGRAFFITO — A decoration produced by dipping an object made with a dark body into a lighter colored slip (or sometimes vice versa) and then scratching through the slip to expose the body.

ENGLISH LUSTRE — A decoration produced by applying a very thin coating of metal to a ceramic object. Platinum becomes "silver", gold becomes the copper colors or shades of rose and pink. Applied to both earthenware and porcelain, and in conjunction with many other decorative techniques.

TRANSFER PRINTING — A process for applying engraved designs to ceramic surfaces, first used by British potters in the eighteenth century. Originally used over the glaze, then underneath, then in many variations.

the British had developed a sophisticated production which could turn out relatively inexpensive ceramics that were very attractive. Try as they would, the American potters, who were in a still less advantageous position than the French, could not compete in their own market.

Ceramics Imported for the American Market — One of the objectives of the American revolution was the freedom to trade where and when we wished. In particular, Americans wanted to trade directly with China instead of through Britain. After the Treaty of Paris was signed in 1783, this wish

Chinese Trade porcelain made for the European market, cup and saucer in a pattern of jugglers and an acrobat, circa 1785. Photograph by Noel Kopald

was realized, with the first American vessel, the "Empress of China", setting sail for Canton; during the years that followed, tons of Chinese porcelain, tea, silk, and the like were imported.

Chinese ceramics made for the American market are usually referred to as "export" ware. Much of the Chinese export porcelain was made to order with personal or patriotic symbols, according to the taste of the clientele. Quite delightful

A remarkably fine Nanking platter, circa 1820–30.
Of the two most familiar Chinese Trade porcelains imported directly to this country (1790–1850) Nanking or Nankeen as it is sometimes called, was the more elaborate and more carefully painted in traditional, river, rocks, bridges, and houses; the similar ware is the plain or Canton.
Photograph by Noel Kopald

were objects which depicted the signers of the Declaration of Independence, all looking very much like Chinese gentlemen. Much more of the Chinese export ware, however, was simply made for the mass market, and it is these wares, the blue and white Canton and Nanking wares and the later Rose Medallion ware, which are the most easily collected today in the Midwest. These porcelains with their underglaze and overglaze hand painting are decorated in Chinese designs; they look especially well when displayed with antique furniture.

Even after independence Americans continued to obtain much of their ceramics from Britain. Some of it, such as Liverpol jugs and Anglo-American historical china, was made especially for the American market. Later, Americans imported Haviland dinner sets from France, as well as a variety of porcelains from the German states. European peasant pottery was also imported, with the result that it is now sometimes difficult to distinguish between the European product and native American earthenware of the type usually associated with Pennsylvania slip and sgraffito ware.

SOME OBSOLETE TERMS THAT CAN BE MISLEADING

SOFT PASTE — This term (without the "porcelain") is used in many old books to refer to a variety of earthenwares, especially those with light bodies such as creamware. It should be used only for porcelain.

LOWESTOFT or ORIENTAL LOWESTOFT — You may encounter this term used to refer to Chinese porcelain. It properly refers to an English Pottery (established 1757) which made soft paste porcelain of a provincial type.

This enormous export market was a response to, as well as a cause of, the lack of American ceramics. It is interesting to note that the first official dinner service, President Washington's, came from China in 1789. It was not until one hundred and twenty four years later that an American president, Woodrow Wilson, was able to have an American dinner service, Lennox, in the White House.

"Hospital Boston" platter from the "Beauties of America" series made for the American trade by John and William Ridgway in Hanley, England, circa 1825. This was the small beginning of Massachusetts General Hospital. The cornerstone was laid in 1818. An excellent example of Anglo-American historical China. Photograph by Noel Kopald

GLASS

Those of you who love glass should be of good cheer, for although glass-making in America had a frustrating start, its rapid development over the last two hundred years has provided the collector with an abundance of opportunities in what has probably become the most popular field in American collecting.

In the seventeenth and eighteenth centuries those colonists who could afford fine glassware had to import their wares from Europe. In the seventeenth century, Venice, France, the German states, and Prague were the chief centers for such glassware, but by the eighteenth century Britain was able to supply most of the quality glassware exported to America. These early imported European glasswares are lovely, but virtually unobtainable on the market today.

Starting with the Jamestown settlement in Virginia in 1608, numerous glass houses, as the early factories were called, were set up in America. Many of these failed, probably because the pressing problems of survival left little time or energy for anything else. Although no authenticated examples of the wares made are available, it seems likely that window glass, bottles, and perhaps everyday drinking glasses accounted for most of the production.

The first notable success in colonial glassmaking came in 1739 when a German, Caspar Wistar, set up a glass house in southern New Jersey and imported skilled glassblowers from his homeland. Window glass and bottles composed the greater part of his output, but it is the so-called "off-hand" pieces, made from the same bottle and window glass, that interest collectors. These were objects made by the glassblowers in off-hours for their families and friends; they consisted of decorative pitchers, bowls, candlesticks, and many other delightful decorative and useful pieces. Many new forms were

English glass sweetmeat dish with cover; heavily leaded, footed, circa 1820; brilliant shallow diamond cuttings. Paid $75; valued at $325.

worked out in this kind of glass that are quite different from European work.

Wistar's factory was closed in 1780 because of the depression brought on by the Revolutionary War. However, the kind of glass produced there continued to be made in South Jersey and, in the nineteenth century, in other parts of the country, as far north as New Hampshire and as far west as Ohio. These pieces of "South Jersey" glass, as it is called regardless of where it is made, are difficult to identify as to maker or place.

Another German, William Henry Stiegel, came to Pennsylvania in the mid-eighteenth century, and soon set up in the glass business; his factory was the first one in the colonies to produce a rather sophisticated glass similar to that made in England and Germany. Stiegel was a flamboyant entrepreneur, and it is possible that overexpansion and personal

---

TYPES OF GLASS

LEAD GLASS — A high quality glass made from oxide of lead, sand with nitre, and black oxide of manganese. It has great refractive power and can be deeply cut.

FLINT GLASS — Another high quality glass that shares all the fine attributes of lead glass but is made with powdered calcined flint instead of lead.

NON-LEAD GLASS — There are many types of non-lead (and non-flint) glasses all of which lack the refractive power of these finer varities. Some common types are **GREEN GLASS, SODA GLASS,** and **LIME GLASS.** These glasses, for the reasons mentioned above, are generally much less expensive than lead or flint glasses.

Flint sugar base in "Plain Octagon" pattern, made in the Midwest (Metz, vol. 1, Early American Pattern Glass #179, page 22), circa 1830–40. This base looks as well without its cover and is typical of good buys in early American flint for use with country furnishings. Sugar bases cost about $25. With covers the cost is about $80.

American celery vase in clear glass with scalloped top edge; this type of object was made in many patterns and variants over a long period of time. This one about mid-nineteenth century. Currently sells for about $55.

extravagance contributed to the collapse of his ventures at about the time of the Revolution. The records indicate that he made both lead and nonlead glass, clear and colored, pattern-molded, free-blown, enameled and engraved. Because of the stylistic similarities, they are difficult to distinguish from the European imports.

John Frederic Amelung, also from Germany, was the last

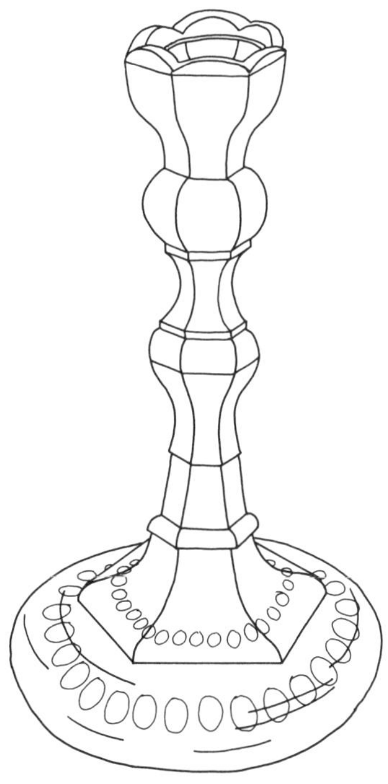

American clear glass candlestick, often called "Colonial-type" (Carl W. D. Depperd: "ABC's of Old Glass", page 129); none were made in colonial times — most were made in the Empire period.

of the glassmakers of the eighteenth century to make a serious effort to set up a stable business in the new republic. Evidently Amelung too had rather extravagant Continental notions of how glass entrepreneurs should conduct their affairs, since by the end of the eighteenth century he, like Stiegel, before him, found himself bankrupt. Be that as it may, Amelung's signed or otherwise identified pieces are the best glass made in eighteenth century America.

Collecting eighteenth century American glass is very difficult; however you will find not only that nineteenth century America is rich in antique glass, but that equally diverse and interesting sorts of glass have been made in the last one hundred years. (We will discuss these in the following chapter on collectibles.)

The new American republic distinguished itself in advancing the technology of glass production, making possible many new kinds of glass. Among them were the revival of an ancient process for making blown three-mold glass and the development of a completely new pressed glass. As Elizabeth Stillinger has stated so eloquently in her invaluable book, *The Antique Guide to Decorative Arts in America:*

> There is probably nothing so uniquely American among the decorative arts as pressed glass. American character is molded into a lacy cup plate just as surely as are its outline and pattern. A kind of pioneer spirit fostered the technical and mechanical know-how that produced machinery for pressing tablewares.[4]

From the early nineteenth century on, pressed glass made up the bulk of American table glass, with pressing machines largely replacing glassblowers. Most of the early pressed glass was called lacy glass because of the overall stippling, or "lace", in the pattern, which compensated for technical problems in the pressing. Once these problems were resolved, around 1840, lacy glass was replaced by what was called pressed-pattern glass, which had a bolder patterning. In addition to tablewares, pressed glass was used to make such objects as lamps, candlesticks, vases, figural bottles and flasks, all of which are quite sought after by collectors.

It would be impossible, of course, to describe here all the kinds and patterns available in nineteenth century glass, but the many good books available on the subject will guide you in looking at museum displays and talking with dealers.

AMERICAN FOLK ART

American folk art is one of the most popular categories in collecting today. Perhaps because of this enormous interest, there is increasing confusion on the part of many as to exactly what it should include.

The following quote from Alice Winchester should give you an excellent idea of the diversity of items that can be considered American folk art:

> The pictures, executed in oil, watercolor, ink, pastel, charcoal, pencil and stitchery, cover a wide range of subject matter: portraits, landscapes and seascapes, scenes of daily life, religious, literary, and historical pieces, still life, and fraktur. The sculpture in wood, metal, stone, and bone includes portraits, ship carvings, weather vanes, shop signs, toys, decoys, and certain household ornaments. Among architectural decorations are the painted overmantels, fireboards, cornices, walls, and floors that once enlivened interiors, and the carving and painting that ornamented exteriors. Certain types of furniture, principally those embellished with painted decoration, and other domestic appurtenances are also treated here.[5]

American folk art may best be defined in terms of the people who created it. These were people who lacked academic schooling or other formal training, such as an apprenticeship in a craft, but who nonetheless made useful objects and decorated them with painting, carving, or by other means, so that these objects had aesthetic as well as utilitarian value. A classic example of folk art practiced by many American women over the centuries is the quilt, which is so popular today with collectors precisely for its decorative rather than for its utilitarian qualities.

Miss Winchester notes that many people seem to think that "folk art includes every sort of household, farm, trade and shop equipment or product that has an unsophisticated or 'country' character."[6] At least some of the confusion in this field exists because many objects which look attractive when displayed with American folk art, such as English spatter-decorated ware, early blown and pattern glass, and Bennington-type pottery and stoneware, are sometimes considered to be folk art. But by definition a factory-made piece cannot be folk art, which is the handwork of individuals. Now that American folk art is so fashionable many objects will, of

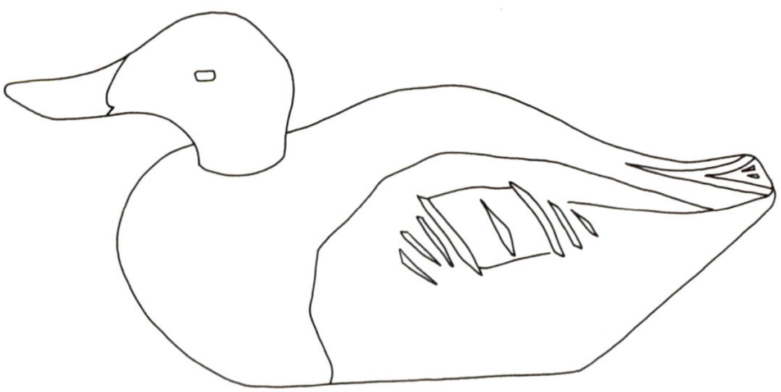

A decoy in original condition and paint; probably Illinois but exact origin unknown.

course, be described indiscriminately as folk art simply to give them an air of importance and to raise their prices.

The interest in American folk art is potentially one of the happiest developments of the last few decades in that it eliminates the unfortunate division between "fine" and "decorative" arts. Moreover, it has encouraged a return to hand crafts, for it has given Americans a sense of a continuing tradition which is still alive and to which they might also contribute.

TRAYS

Trays are available in a variety of sizes and materials, including metal, papier mâché and wood. The metal and papier mâché trays are often japanned (that is, finished with varnishes, paint and gilding in imitation of Oriental lacquers) in numerous decorative styles. Wooden trays can also be quite attractive, particularly those made of figured mahogany. Trays can be very useful as well as decorative, especially when mounted on stands so that they can be used as small occasional tables. This is often an ideal solution to the problem of providing a period room with a compatible coffee table.

PEWTER AND BRITANNIA

Pewter is an alloy made of varying proportions of tin and copper; lead, antimony or bismuth are sometimes added for greater workability or economy. The better grades of pewter have a high ratio of tin to copper and no lead. The adoption of pewter for domestic use, which became widespread

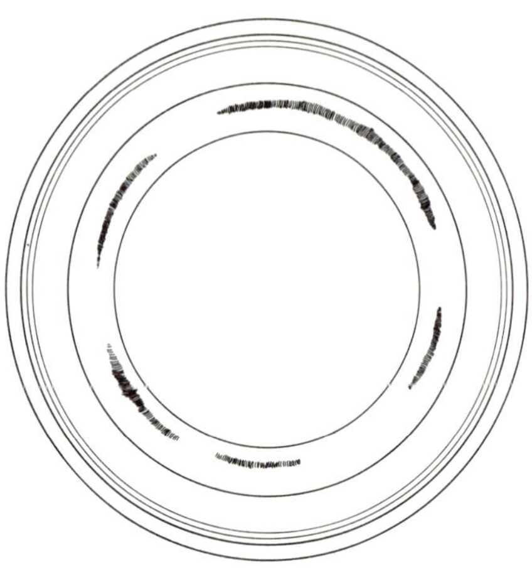

Elegant simplicity characterizes this shallow pewter dish, 14⅞″ in diameter. Made in the late eighteenth century. Sold for $160. If this dish had an American mark its monetary value would be greatly increased. Much pewter, American and British, is unmarked.

---

both on the American continent and in Europe by the mid-eighteenth century, represented a great improvement in appearance and sanitation over the wooden trenchers, mugs and spoons which previously were in common use. Pewter continued to be prominent in the field of tablewares for about a century, at which time it was displaced by ceramics and silver.

Pewter is fragile, easily damaged by any but the most careful handling, quickly worn out, and destroyed by heat. Nonetheless, good pieces look very attractive when displayed with early pottery such as sgraffito, slipware or delft.

Careful study and a knowledgeable dealer are a must for the collector for two reasons. First, identification is sometimes difficult, since marking is inconsistent for both American and British pewter. Second, prices have been so high in the last few years that fakes in the marketplace are almost inevitable.

Britannia was a superior form of pewter from a technological standpoint: it was not fragile, it could be machine rolled into sheets and spun on a lathe. It contained no lead and could be successfully engraved. It was made into many shapes during its short life in high public favor in the United States, namely from 1830 to about 1860, when it was displaced by electroplated silver.

THE OTHER METALS:
IRON, BRASS, COPPER, AND TIN

Many metals played important roles in colonial households. Cast and wrought iron were necessary to provision the fireplace, which was used not only for cooking but also for heat

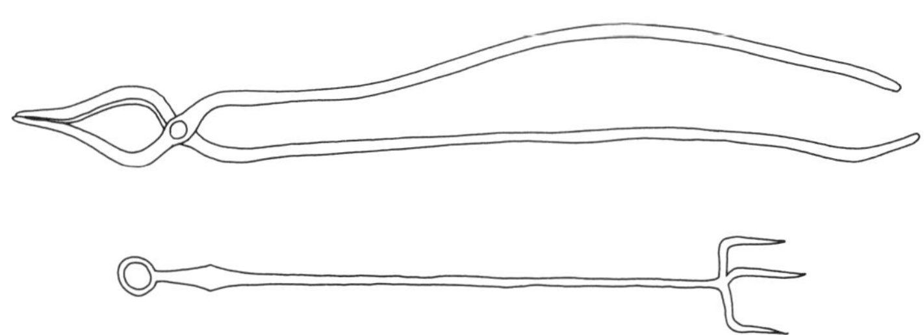

American wrought iron tongs, eighteenth century.
English flesh fork, eighteenth century.

and much of the light in early generations. Iron was used for grates, firebacks, andirons and fire tools. It was also needed for pots, teakettles and other vessels as well as for hooks, trammels and other cooking implements around the fireplace. It was used for a whole host of essential items, from candlestands, latches and weathervanes, to the tools necessary for the household and for the trades.

From the mid-eighteenth century cast iron was used for the famous Franklin stove — one of the early efforts to provide more efficient home heating. By the mid-nineteenth century the advances of industrialization brought the first steam-heated building to the United States, the Eastern Hotel of Boston, but to many modest homes across the nation it brought cast iron cooking ranges and parlor stoves.

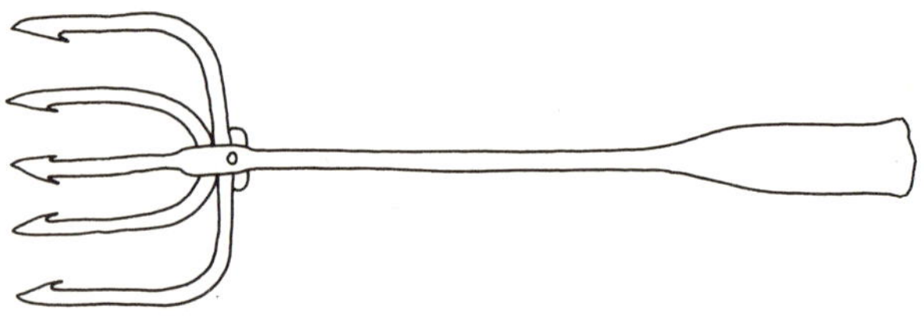

American wrought iron fish spear, nineteenth century.

Brass, copper and tin were also a valued part of early households. They were made into a variety of useful kitchen utensils as well as numerous other small objects. Brass was a particularly desired accessory in more affluent households, and much of it was imported in the form of candlesticks, chandeliers, andirons, furniture brasses and other objects.

Very few American-made metals of the pre-revolutionary period are available. Many if not most of the metals used in colonial America were actually of British manufacture. These objects received hard use and when they were worn out were either discarded or reworked into other objects. Most of the identifiably eighteenth-century metals now available for sale are items such as brass candlesticks and chandeliers which are European in origin. If you plan to buy metals of the

English brass, late eighteenth century, candlestick. An unusual feature is the British coin "1786" used in the "push up". The push up is a very simple and practical device making it possible to burn the candles (always expensive) down to the end.

English brass candlestick made in late seventeenth or the first half of the eighteenth centuries. A very desirable type, it can be found in the Midwest.

eighteenth or early nineteenth century, be prepared to do some research first. These objects are usually expensive, and you will want to know just what you are buying.

From the nineteenth century on there are many more objects available, but you need to remember that it is often difficult to date metals or to determine just where they were made. Among the nineteenth-century metals you can find most easily are cast iron stoves, candlesticks in brass, iron and tin, a variety of tools, and some cooking and fireplace equipment.

In particular, American tinware in its plain, punched and painted forms is not difficult to find and looks very attractive with country furniture. Unfortunately the prices of these charming objects, which composed such a considerable part of the stock of the famous "Yankee peddlers", have soared in recent years. Making and decorating tinware are crafts quite within the abilities of many of us — a good thing to remember perhaps before deciding to buy a painted tin coffee pot whose price runs into four figures.

TEXTILES

Textiles, from window, bed, and wall hangings to lace, embroideries, quilts, coverlets, bedspreads, upholstery fabrics and rugs, form a large category of objects which were an essential part of past domestic life. Unfortunately textiles are particularly fragile, and if used for the purposes for which they were originally intended their life is rather short. We are fortunate in that many of these delightful objects were very highly regarded by their original owners, and for this reason received careful handling and little use, making them available to us today. The question remains: how to display and enjoy them and at the same time preserve them for future generations.

When appropriate, as in the case of the needlework pictures of the eighteenth and early nineteenth centuries, framing is an ideal solution. Framing is also appropriate for the woven silk Stevensgraphs of the Victorian period and can even be used for the fragile silk crazy quilts of the same period, which make surprisingly beautiful wall decorations. I have also seen fragments of fine fabrics and laces framed in such a way that they make lovely additions to their owners' decors.

It is important to frame properly, however. Because textiles are particularly susceptible to fading from light, you should use only glass wihch screens out the ultraviolet rays, and avoid hanging textiles where there is direct sunlight. As in framing works of art on paper, you should of course use only acid-free materials. The framing of textiles differs from graphics, mainly in that it is often considered wise, especially where mildewing might be a problem, to permit more air circulation, usually by not completely sealing the back. Especially if the work is valuable, you will want to make sure it is competently framed.

4

Survey of the Field: **COLLECTIBLES**

Between the founding of our country and 1875, the date that divides the antiques from the collectibles, the American population had increased from less than four million to over fifty million. By 1900 the American population was almost 76 million; by 1950 it was over 150 million. These statistics are important for they help to explain the availability and the prices of the objects we wish to collect. Generally speaking, objects from the period of collectibles exist in much greater abundance than earlier objects. The Midwest was well settled by 1875, and objects from this period were made in great quantities. Except for a few things which were made in very limited numbers and thus always were rare, collectibles can easily be found in this section of the country.

Factory-made kitchen cupboard in maple, circa 1890. The various drawers and bins provided convenient storage for yesterday's housewife. Today, they enliven modern kitchens, while retaining their usefulness. Bought from dealer for $125.

91

By 1875 the simple agrarian economy of the early republic had been all but replaced by a rapidly expanding industrial economy, and the nation was well on its way to becoming a great world power. By this time the United States shared with the older, imperial powers of Europe the belief in a world of limitless material wealth that was theirs for the taking, then and always. This conviction could not but put its stamp upon the whole character of the Victorian period, including its decorative arts, which are marked by a preference for elaborate ornament, eclectic design, and massive scale.

The Victorian taste for luxury and comfort as well as the delight in novelty and the exoticism of far-off places were all part of the rising affluence and expectations of the new middle classes. The post-Civil War period had created a whole new class of people eager for the better things of life, and mechanization in all the crafts not only made it possible to supply an abundance of goods, but also made it temptingly easy to turn out elaborate ornamental detail which could substitute for good basic design.

In earlier days design was controlled by the traditional training that guided craftsmen and by the educated taste of a limited elite who set the standards for gracious living. The new elite of the post-Civil War period, the industrialists, bankers and politicians, lacked the cultural rootedness of America's earlier leaders and they were unable to provide the sort of aesthetic guidance that might have resulted in better design, suitable for machine production. In fact they were much more easily pleased than the older elite, and in their haste to achieve the trappings of their new status they did what is usual with the newly rich: they looked backward to symbols of grandeur borrowed indiscriminately from the past. This free-floating urge for whatever would look impressive accelerated the eclecticism in architecture and interior decoration that had been growing in the Victorian era. The guid-

Meridienne in French Empire style, probably designed for an 1880s furniture exhibition in Europe. Made of mahogany with unusually fine Dutch-style marquetry. The skills necessary for this exacting craft have almost disappeared, but fortunately, much furniture embellished with marquetry was made in various styles in the second half of the nineteenth century. Examples can be found occasionally in the Midwest.

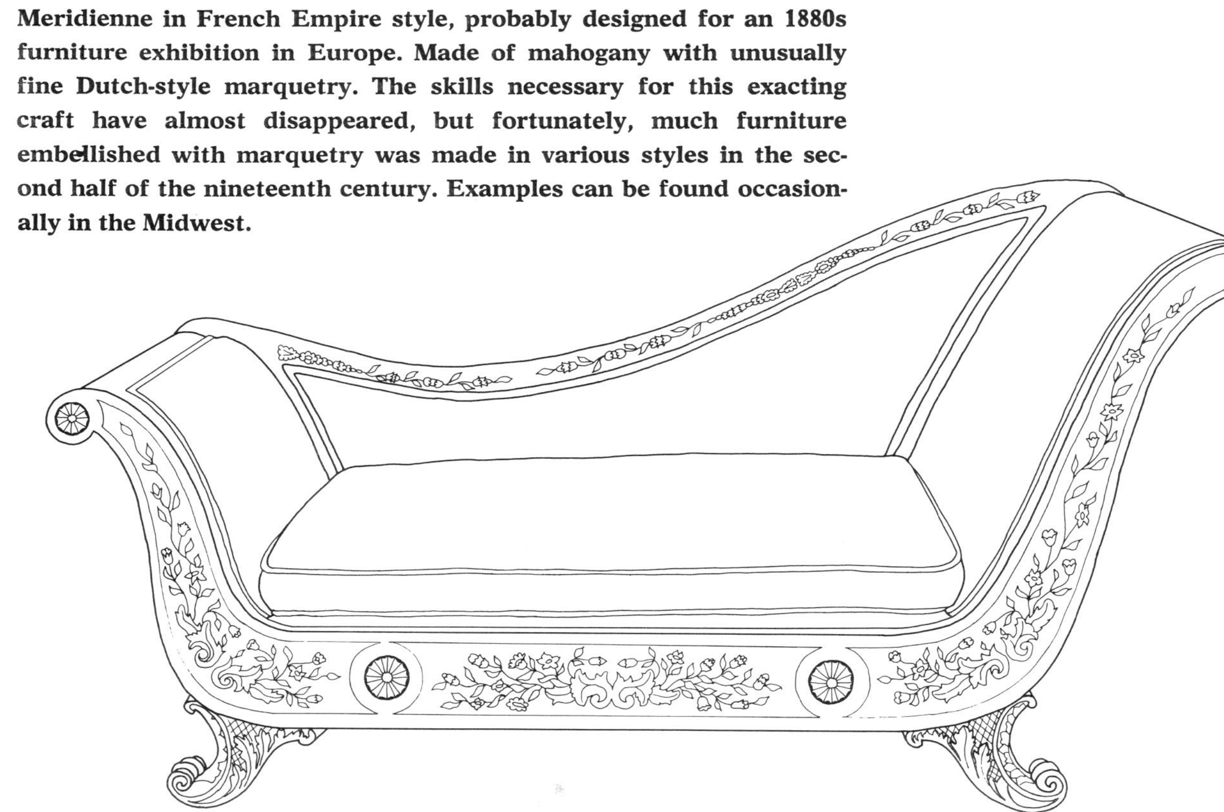

ing principle seemed to be "if a little is good, a lot is better", resulting in a great increase in the size of houses and in the proportions of their furnishings. In the cottages and houses of moderate size as well as in the large establishments, the "full furnished" fashion prevailed.

FURNITURE

Late Victorian Eclecticism — American furniture styles of the last quarter of the nineteenth century included the following revivals: Louis XIV, XV, XVI, First Empire, Renaissance, and American "colonial", as well as the more exotic Turkish, Moorish, Egyptian and Japanese styles. This incomplete list of revivals and adaptations does not adequately convey the eclecticism with which styles borrowed from the past were used; more often than not decorative motifs from several styles would be combined with little regard for historical accuracy in a single object. The newly rich in America, like their counterparts elsewhere, seemed to find reassurance in multiple stamps of approval of their taste.

I do not mean to suggest, however, that you should ignore the furniture of this period. There are few periods of decorative art without objects of interest and value, and the remarkable diversity of the furniture made here from 1875 to 1940 should provide something for almost everyone. In sorting out the various styles, you are likely to find many things that will please you.

As you study the late Victorian era, you will discover that one of its novelties is that not all its furniture is made of wood. The inventiveness and interest in the exotic which characterized the whole era both here and abroad led to a great deal of experimentation with new materials for making furniture. Iron, used mainly in hallstands and garden furniture, was one innovation; as a material for garden furniture

94

it is still quite popular today. Papier-mâché, used mainly for small occasional pieces, had a much shorter life and was generally imported.

A uniquely American contribution inspired by the West was the use of elk, buffalo and steer horns to make furniture, usually chairs, sofas, stools, and hatracks. If you are interested in this very unusual furniture, examples do sometimes turn up in the Midwest. Horn furniture was quite popular in the late nineteenth and early twentieth centuries.

Other Victorian experiments were so practical and attractive that they are still being used today. Among these are bentwood, wicker, and bamboo furniture, which were made here after being introduced from abroad. Bentwood was most often made into chairs and rockers; wicker into chairs, tables, and other small pieces; and bamboo into a variety of small forms, including bookcases. Wooden furniture which simulated bamboo was also made. These forms have retained their popularity because they are lightweight, remarkably sturdy, and attractive. They are all available in the Midwest.

Despite these interesting innovations in the use of materials, the bulk of furniture made in this period continued to be of wood, worked in traditional ways. Most home-owners looked for novelty less in the working of furniture than in the profusion of styles in which it was available — a profusion which even a skilled antiquarian could hardly be expected to keep straight. In this period, there was an outpouring of advice on how to furnish one's home, the gist of which was usually to have a little of everything. Typical of such advice was the suggestion of one contemporary that

> among the designs that were to be considered before a home could be properly and fashionably furnished were those in the Gothic, Renaissance, Elizabethan, Jacobean, Louis XVI, Pompeian, Moorish, Eastlake, Queen Anne, Oriental and modern styles.[7]

If the railroad builders, industrialists and financiers had some difficulties in following this advice to the letter, you can imagine the situation of less affluent Americans in this perennial problem of keeping up with the Joneses.

Several ranks below the tycoons and well-to-do, people of very modest means were able to have furniture and other household effects that were greatly simpilfied versions of those already described. Mass production techniques were used effectively to produce inexpensive goods which, with new

A delightful primitive elm dropleaf table. No wonder they were made over many decades. Bought at a house sale for $5.

ways of merchandising, could find new markets. Advertising became more enticing and insistent. By the end of the nineteenth century the mail-order houses were performing their function of changing American life-styles to fit the seemingly endless capacity of industry to produce consumer goods. Again, with some sorting out, collectors can find things from this period that are both useful and pleasing. The quality of workmanship and the materials used, whether solid wood or veneer on solid wood, are a far cry from the remarkable shoddiness of so much of today's furniture.

The effects of the industrial revolution on the decorative arts were first criticized in Britain, where the problems following in the wake of mass production had had the most time to accumulate. The art critic John Ruskin, the artist William Morris, and other Victorians considered machine production dehumanizing and believed that machine-made objects could not but have an adverse effect on public morals. These pre-Raphaelites, as they called themselves, produced some very beautiful furniture, but their work was much too expensive to influence people generally and too restrained and avant-garde to appeal to the wealthy. Their ideas, generations later, had some effect on modern furniture design. The most tangible result of their work was the Morris chair, which was first made by a company Morris himself founded, and which continued to be made in quantity in the United States for over fifty years.

Although the ideas of Ruskin and other critics were seriously considered in the United States, it was a book by another reformer, Charles Eastlake's *Hints on Household Taste,* that had the greatest impact on the thinking and taste of Americans. Eastlake's book was so popular with Americans that it went through eight editions from 1872 to 1890. Eastlake was an architect, and although he designed some furniture, his book made clear that he was primarily concerned with the moral principles that furniture should embody, such as "sincerity of purpose", "constructive principles", and "simplicity". Unfortunately his name has been associated indiscriminately with monstrosities as well as with finely made furniture and inexpensive, restrained cottage-type furniture. "Eastlake" furniture is abundant in the Midwest.

Eastlake gilded walnut mirror of the more restrained and agreeable sort, circa 1875–80; combines well with restrained Empire and Victorian furniture. Found in an alley.

98

Art Nouveau, Arts and Crafts, "Mission" — There were two very different responses to the criticism raised by people such as Ruskin, Morris and Eastlake. One was the Arts and Crafts movement and the other was Art Nouveau. Both movements were experimental, both wanted to break away from what they saw as the degraded design of the late Victorian era. But their decorative styles were very different.

Art Nouveau, which originated in Europe and reached its fullest development in architecture and furniture there, was elegant, ornamental and curvilinear. It flowered in the two decades before and after the turn of the century. Although furniture in this style is occasionally found here, the better pieces are usually expensive.

The Arts and Crafts movement, which began in the last quarter of the nineteenth century and as a movement was most active in England, favored a functional simplicity in line and ornament. But like the earlier critics of Victorian design, the leaders of this movement disliked machine production, and their romanticization of handcraftsmanship prevented them from solving the problem of providing soundly designed objects for the general public.

The most significant exception to this failure of the Arts and Crafts movement was the "Mission" furniture originated in the United States by Gustav Stickley at the end of the nineteenth century. Stickley's ideas of what furniture should be are plainly stated in one of his advertisements:

> The piece is first, last and all the time a chair, and not an imitation of a throne, nor an exhibit of snakes and dragons in a wild riot of misapplied wood-carving. The fundamental purpose in building this chair was to make a piece which should be essentially comfortable, durable, well proportioned and as soundly put together as the best workmanship, tools and materials made possible.[8]

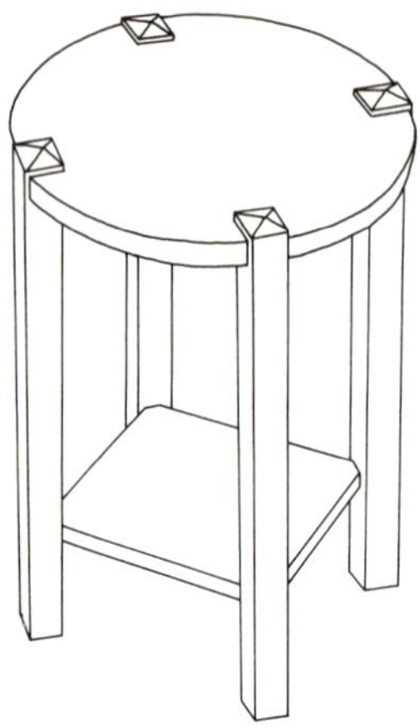

**Arts and Crafts oak plant stand with shelf, circa 1900–15.
Free from a junk dealer.**

His rather massive oak furniture, so suited to mass production, was plain, angular and very solid. Mission furniture was so popular in America for the first two decades of the twentieth century that it still exists in considerable abundance.

The ideas of the Arts and Crafts movement which led into Mission furniture evolved into various sorts of modern furniture designs which broke with the traditions of eighteenth and nineteenth century design. Among those influenced by the Arts and Crafts movement were Frank Lloyd Wright and other members of the "Prairie School". Wright and others of his school designed relatively little furniture, though pieces are occasionally found in the Midwest.

Art Deco — Art Deco takes its name from the "Exposition Internationale des Arts Décoratifs et Industriels Modernes" which was held in Paris in 1925. The modernist objects we

Le Corbusier, French, adjustable chaise lounge; made in 1929. Courtesy of the Art Institute of Chicago; bequest of Hedwig B. Schniewind. This example of the avant--garde trend in Art Deco was restored by Jens Simonsgaard, my husband, in the early sixties. He had only the base and the tubular steel frame, but no information about how the foundation for the steer hide had been made. Mrs. Schniewind and he were delighted when he solved the problem. The bolster was added later.

associate with the term Art Deco actually made up only a small part of the styles on display at this famous exhibition. It is important to remember that the period of Art Deco, 1920 to 1940, was one of diverse styles.

There were two main trends during this period; the first might be described as traditionalist, the other as modernist. First, there were cabinet makers, silversmiths, and other designers who worked in the traditional manner of eighteenth and nineteenth century craftsmen. Though their work shows the influence of modern, simplified design, their use of traditional methods of craftsmanship inevitably resulted in their work also showing the stylistic influence of earlier periods. Some of the furniture they made was quite plain, some of it was very ornate; in either case it was meant to convey elegance and style. Visually much of it bears some resemblance to esoteric versions of Empire furniture. Like the luxurious silver, glass and other work of these craftsmen, this highly decorative furniture was meticulously made of opulent materials and was so costly that it was intended only for a very wealthy clintele.

The "high-style" work of the traditionalists predominated at the Exposition, but the modernist styles probably had the more lasting influence on twentieth century design. The modernist trend, which was characterized by a self-conscious break with tradition, was geometric and spare in line. It was designed for mass production so that it could be made available to many people, and was conceived as an appropriate response to the increasingly mechanized world of the twentieth century.

The high-style, traditionalist furniture is not easy to find. It was always made in very small amounts to special order and therefore was very expensive; moreover, it is now very much in fashion. The modernist style is much more available, but you still may have quite a search to find it.

102

Edgar Brandt, French, console table, wrought and welded steel, brêche d'Aleps marble top and base, circa 1925. Courtesy of the Art Institute of Chicago; Russell Tyson Fund. This table represents the high-style work of the traditionalist designers in Art Deco.

SILVER

American Silver — By the end of the Civil War the hand-craftsmanship of individual silversmiths had largely been replaced by the increasingly mechanized production of large companies. As with the furniture of the collectible period, styles and decorative techniques in silver changed rapidly; the taste of the clintele as well as the offerings of the manufacturers were quite volatile.

An incredible array of decorative styles were revived in silver, such as rococo, Gothic, Elizabethan, Renaissance and classical. Others were newly invented, such as "Oriental", "Assyrian", and "Indian". And again, as with the furniture of this period, these varied styles were often combined with little regard for decorative consistency. Some of the aesthetic ventures of the late nineteenth century in silver were of course more successful than others.

With the discovery of silver in the West, there were vast new quantities of silver available, and at the same time there was a new class of very wealthy people with a desire for opulent living and the status that silver could provide. As a result there was an enormous increase in the number and types of silver objects produced, as well as in the ornateness of designs. The very wealthy had extensive and elaborate dinner services which sometimes included goblets, plates, and serving dishes as well as flatware for every course and each different food. There also were elaborate centerpieces and other objects which were purely ornamental. Some of the solely decorative silver made on special order for the very wealthy in the late nineteenth century combined already elaborate silver work with enameling and semiprecious stones, thus making luxurious and opulent objects that fitted well into the extremely ornate decors which were the fashion of that time.

Art Nouveau silver was made by many American manufacturers, both large and small, in the period from 1895 to 1910. There were a great variety of types made; flatware, sets of spoons, vanity sets, and numerous small pieces that ranged from hairpins to matchboxes. This silver was also made in a variety of ways. Many relatively inexpensive sets were stamped out in the thousands by machines. At the other extreme was Gorham's completely handmade Martelé silver, all of which was made of 950/1000 metal with no two pieces alike. Martelé was very expensive even when it was first produced and it is seldom found for sale. However, a study of Art Nouveau silver should be of help in buying it on those rare occasions when you can find it.

You will discover that throughout the collectible period much attractive silver was made which is still quite appropriate for use in today's homes and on today's dining tables. There are quantities of old sets of knives, forks, and spoons as well as some complete sets of excellent machine-made flat-

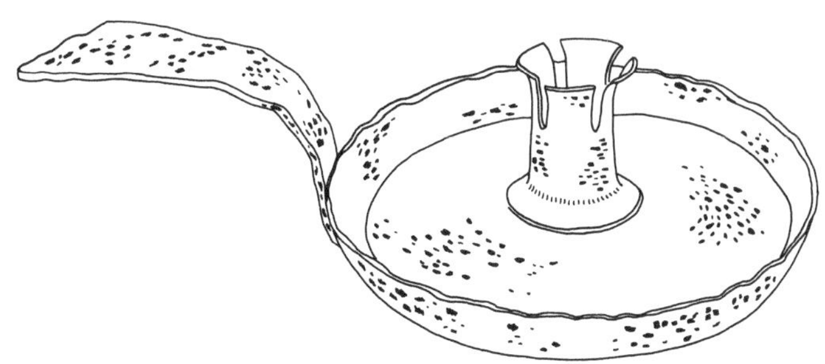

Arts and Crafts chamber stick of beaten silver made by Howard & Co., New York, N.Y., circa 1905. Bought for $110.

ware, hollowware, and various small sterling pieces too numerous to mention. It is good to know that even silver made largely by machine acquires a patina with careful use and correct polishing. The books in the bibliography should help you sort out the different styles and types of pieces made.

The Kalo Shop — From the early twentieth century the Kalo Shop produced excellent handmade silver in Illinois, first in Park Ridge, and then for several generations in Chicago. Only a few years ago it was forced to close, not for lack of clientele but because craftsmen in silver could no longer be found. The apprentice system, long dead insofar as the decorative arts are concerned, obviously will have to be resumed in some degree if we mean to continue this form of art.

During the years of their operation, the Kalo Shop made many types of small objects, usually to special order, such. as bowls, pitchers, goblets, small boxes, flatware, and jewelry.

This modern version of the porringer was made for "Peggy" at the Kalo Shop in Chicago in this century.

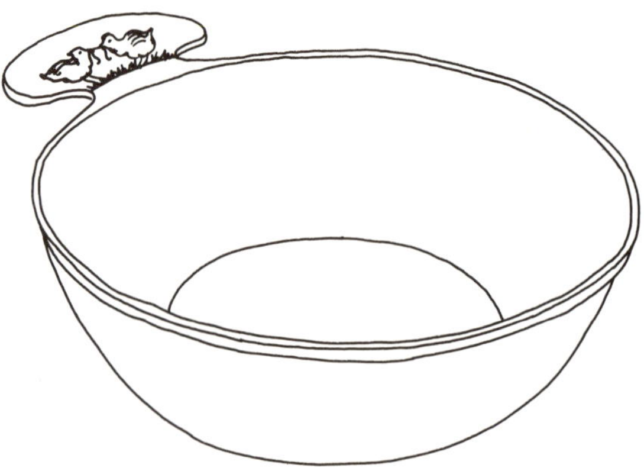

The signature, so to speak, of their workmanship was the process of hand-beating which gives the surfaces of their objects a distinctive texture and beauty. Silver objects made in the Kalo Shop are eagerly sought by collectors, and can be found in the Midwest.

Electroplated Silver — This new and cheaper method of plating silver, developed in England, put silver within the range of almost every pocketbook. It first came to the United States in the 1840s, and after the Civil War it was made in enormous quantities. You can find innumerable objects of Victorian electroplated silver; some of them are quite attractive and they are not expensive. Some collectors buy pieces with worn plating and have the remaining silver removed;

Figural napkin ring with an unusually well-designed owl. Made by the New Bedford Silver Plate Co. in the last quarter of the nineteenth century.

this process is called "skinning". It is a particularly satisfactory method for those pieces having a Britannia base, for what you have after skinning is an object of a hard, silvery pewter. Plated silver varies in quality depending on the amount of silver used in the plating. Most plated silver has marks which indicate the quality of plate. There are books available which explain the various marking systems.

CERAMICS

Although many attractive and useful ceramics have been made in the last 100 years, this period taken as a whole lacks the excitement of continuous experimentation which characterized the period from 1750 to 1850, the most creative period in the whole history of Western ceramics. By the middle of the nineteenth century mechanization in ceramics was well developed. Because of the restraints imposed by the increased size and mechanization of factories, the originality that comes from experimentation was confined in this period for the most part to art pottery which was made either by individual potters or by small concerns.

American Ceramics — After the Centennial there was much more American pottery and porcelain available, especially in decorative objects as well as everyday wares. Here we can only indicate some of the more interesting types.

In the Midwest the firm Knowles, Taylor and Knowles, which got its start in Ohio in the mid-nineteenth century, was making white granite ware by the 1870s. They also made Belleek, a thin china with a lustrous glaze which sometimes was slightly iridescent, and another porcelain, lotus ware, which was often very heavily decorated and quite expensive. They are all available in the Midwest.

In the early twentieth century the Dedham Pottery of Chelsea, Massachusetts made one of its best known wares, which had a crackled glaze and very unusual borders of animals, birds or flowers. At about the same time the Buffalo Pottery of Buffalo, New York, made historical pitchers and plates. It is very well known for its Deldare wares which were made in a distinctive olive green color and often decorated with "Old English" scenes. Both Dedham and Deldare are available though they are both quite expensive.

American Art Pottery — Art pottery has its origins in the Victorian fascination with the purely ornamental. First made in the later nineteenth century, it was meant as a free expression of decorative artistry. Art pottery was made in small quantities by small companies, small groups of potters or individuals; the objects made are almost always decorative, one-of-a-kind wares in forms such as vases, bowls, and candlesticks.

Ohio was particularly distinguished for its art pottery. The Rookwood pottery, the most famous of American art potteries, was established at Cincinnati in 1880. At about the same time there were three well-known art potteries in Zanesville, Ohio: Samuel Weller, J. B. Owens, and the Roseville Pottery Company. Zanesville also had several smaller potteries and tile companies, two of the latter being the American Encaustic Tiling Company and the Mosaic Tile Company. Also of note in the Midwest was the Redwing Art Pottery, established in the early twentieth century in Redwing, Minnesota.

Art pottery was of course made in places other than the Midwest. It would be impossible to list them all, but one especially worthy of note is the Newcomb Pottery at Sophie Newcomb College in New Orleans, active during the first half of the twentieth century.

Art nouveau procelain plate with an opalescent border painted in gold with stylized flowers. Signed on back "ANick 1914". Bought for $1.

Imported Ceramics — For dinnerwares as well as decorative objects, Americans after the Centennial continued to obtain much of their ceramics from Europe. One of the most popular wares was Haviland. It is well known that many, many American middle class families had dinner sets of this porcelain for "best", starting well before 1875 but continuing long after this date. The continuing popularity of Haviland has always been in its dainty charm and in its relatively low cost.

There are specialist dealers in the Midwest who can help you get off to a good start in collecting Haviland, or in filling out old sets.

In the late nineteenth century much decorative and useful porcelain was made in Germany and Austria, as well as in England and elsewhere, for the American trade. Available in the market today are objects from the following factories:

Royal Bayreuth. Made in Germany. Many types of decorative wares were made.

Royal Rudolstadt. Made in Germany. Many types of wares. Its prices are more moderate than some.

R.S. Germany. Made in Tillowitz, Germany. Also many types of wares. It usually is less expensive than the following porcelain:

R.S. Prussia. Made in the same factory as the above. Be careful in buying it because there are many reproductions on the market.

Royal Vienna. Almost all of the Royal Vienna now available has been made by various Austrian and German factories. These wares bear the early shield or beehive mark which was used on the famous Vienna ceramics of the eighteenth century, but these later ceramics are clearly in the styles of the late nineteenth century and should confuse no one familiar with these styles.

Royal Dux. Made in Czechoslovakia in the early twentieth century. Decorative pottery. Again, be cautious; there are reproductions.

Royal Worcester. Made in England under this name since 1862. The factory is still in operation. This ware follows the elaborately decorative styles of the late nineteenth century.

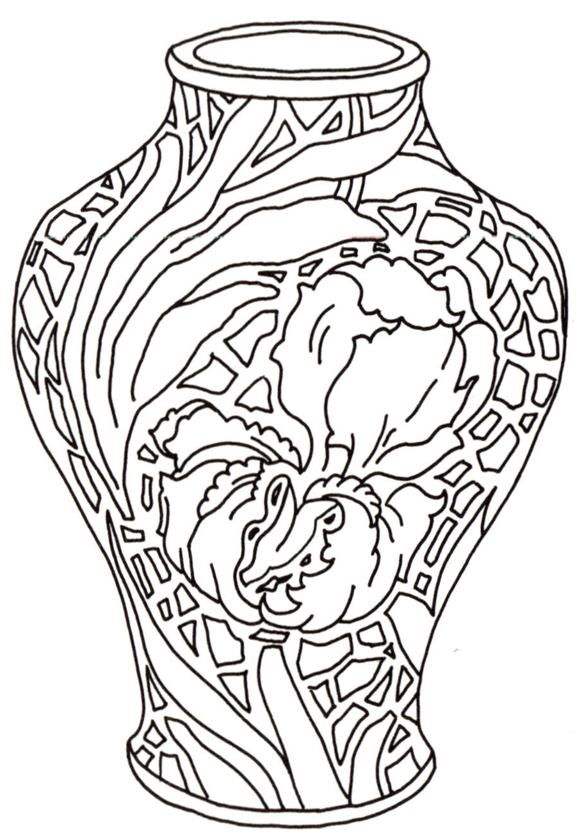

European art nouveau ceramic vase, background brilliant cobalt blue and green; the design is outlined in golden yellow; the irises are blue gray with touches of lavender and yellow, 7⅝" high.

Derby Crown Porcelain Company, Ltd. Made in England. The company was established between 1875 and 1880.

Royal Doulton. Made in England. This name was used after 1902. The factory is still in operation. Many types of decorative wares were made in the medium price range.

Royal Copenhagen. Made in Denmark. The factory, founded in 1772, is still in operation. This ware is expensive and good. In the late nineteenth and twentieth centuries figurines, vases and other decorative wares were made, usually in distinctively grayed colors. The Christmas plate series, which started in 1908, are well-known, and its world-famous "Flora Danica" porcelain is still being made to order.

GLASS

The remarkable developments in American glass making that characterized the earlier part of the nineteenth century continued after the 1870s. The number of new styles and types of glass, as well as the tremendously increased technical facility which they displayed, are truly remarkable. In the late nineteenth century there was internationally an enormous interest in glassmaking, and in many areas the United States led the way. The quantity and quality of American glass made in this period is impressive indeed.

Pattern Glass — Because of the need to conserve lead during the Civil War, most glasswares made then were unleaded, and this practice was continued after the war. Though pattern glass continued to be made in great quantities in the post-war period, it was usually made of lime and soda ash.

Satin glass shoe made by Gillinder & Sons of Philadelphia in the glassworks they erected on the Centennial grounds in 1876 in Philadelphia. This shoe has flowers and leaves painted on the toe. "Gillinder & Sons Philadelphia Exhibition" embossed inside the shoe. These were made in great quantities, and currently sell for about $32.

Before the war most pattern glass was clear; afterwards a wide range of colors was offered, as well as a greatly increased variety of patterns which were usually more elaborate than in the ante bellum period. The pattern glass of this period provides a huge and rewarding field for the collector; but it requires careful study and a knowledgeable dealer, for there are many reproductions.

American Brilliant Period Cut Glass — "Brilliant Period" is the well chosen name for this sparkling, heavily leaded glass made in America from 1880 to 1915. In order to sustain the deep over-all cutting which gave it great refractive power,

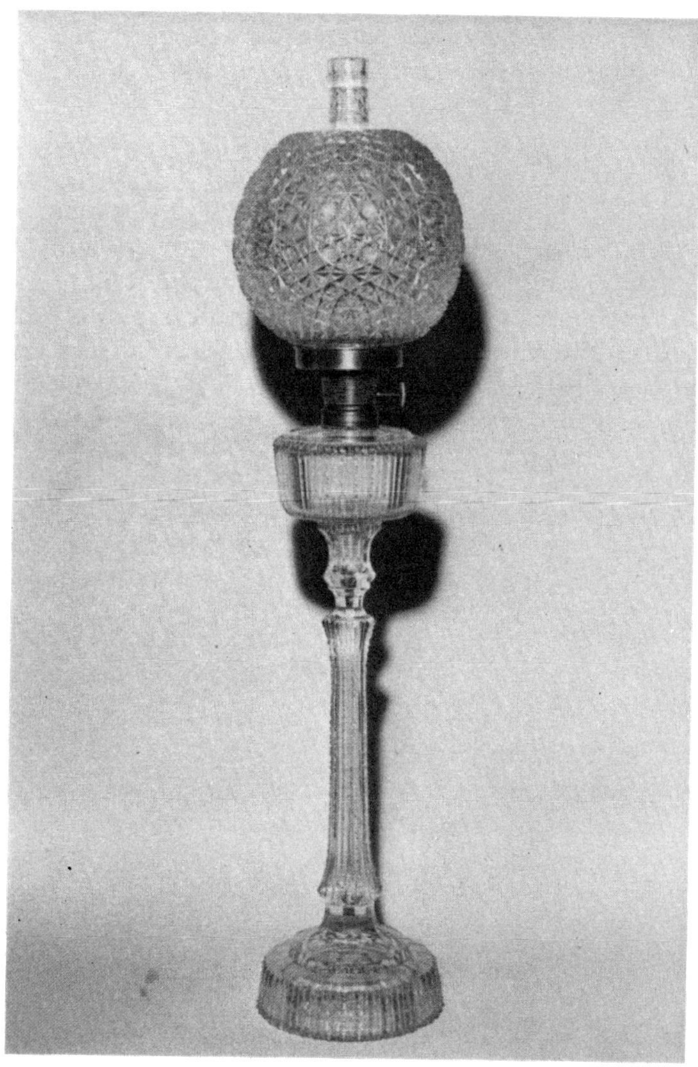

**American brilliant period cut glass lamp, Russian pattern.
Sold at auction in 1974 for $1,200. Photograph courtesy of C. P.
Terry Dunning of Dunning's Auction Service, Elgin, Illinois.**

it had to be made from heavy blanks. This glass has a smooth interior, the sharp cutting being on the outside. Skilled glass cutters used the technological developments which provided the flawless "metal", as glass is called, and the then-new cutting machinery to produce the dazzling objects that so perfectly fitted the ostentatious life styles of the period. Fortunately for collectors, this glass is very difficult to reproduce successfully. It requires great expertise to cut glass, and moreover, high quality lead glass, which is expensive, must be used. But caution is still required in buying because the Czechoslovakians are now making a cut glass which often is completely polished, making it look similar to American brilliant cut glass. Unless you know American glass quite well, you may confuse the two.

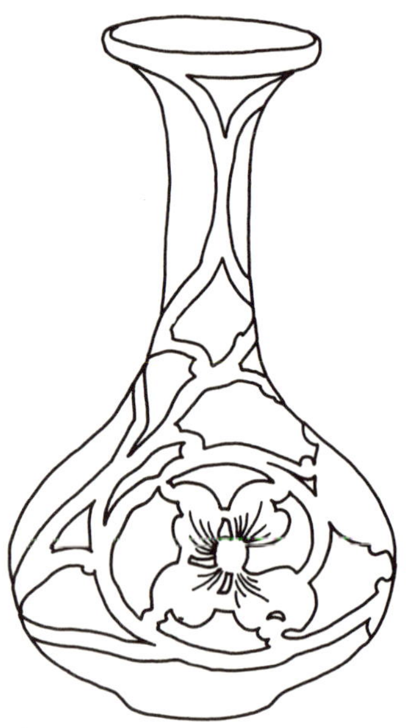

Art nouveau green glass vase, silver overlay, circa 1890.

American Art Glass — Generally speaking, American art glass is among the best made in the world. It is remarkable for its technical excellence, having profited from much experimentation in shape, color, and decorative technique. With some exceptions, the designs are Victorian or Art Nouveau in inspiration. Art glass is very expensive and very much copied. In fact some of the copies made only a few years ago are now being collected in their own right.

The best way to study art glass is to use the many excellent specialized books on the subject; the graphic material these books provide, especially the illustrations in color, will make it easy for you to identify the various types when you see them in shops and shows. A competent dealer is a must for this category.

The best general advice on collecting glass remains that of Carl Drepperd, from the *A B C's of Old Glass:*

> You can collect old blown glass if you want to. You can collect combinations of pressed and blown glass. You can even collect modern reproductions of early glass. One of the first things you should do in becoming a collector is to study and study and restudy all of the modern reproductions and read all the literature you can on the subject. There is no fun in being fooled. Thousands of people are being fooled today by reproductions of blown glassware, blown-mold glassware, two-, three-, and four-pattern mold glass. The majority of these wares are not made to fool the public. They are sold by manufacturers and their agents to the glass and china stores, and to gift shops as legitimate present-day items. It is only when antique shops offer these wares at from two to twenty times the gift-shop price that the sale of reproductions of glassware becomes a racket.[9]

These comments of Drepperd are even more true now than when they were written over twenty-five years ago. More and better reproductions of most types of glass have been made. It is essential to be able to tell the old from the new, the handmade or partially handmade from the completely machine made (where all the materials are placed in the machine and it does the rest). Perhaps this challenge adds to the great fascination that glass has always had, especially for Americans.

Obelisk shaped blue glass paperweight which once had a thermometer in a niche on one side. Aesthetically, it is probably better without it. On two sides of the obelisk are well-painted, handsomely-dressed chinoiserie figures. Date unknown.

American Indian Arts and Crafts

The pottery, weaving, stone carvings, baskets, jewelry and other artifacts of the American Indian, whether made now or in the past, have recently become extremely popular with collectors. For those who are new to this area of interest, there are a few important considerations: 1) Since this category is extremely fashionable, It can require rather substantial sums of money. 2) It is essential to know something about the creator of these arts and crafts in order to have a true understanding of the objects you may wish to buy. 3) Because there is such an abundance of badly designed, machine-made pieces and other fakes made both here and abroad for the "American market", you will find a knowledgeable dealer as well as self education are essential to avoid making expensive mistakes.

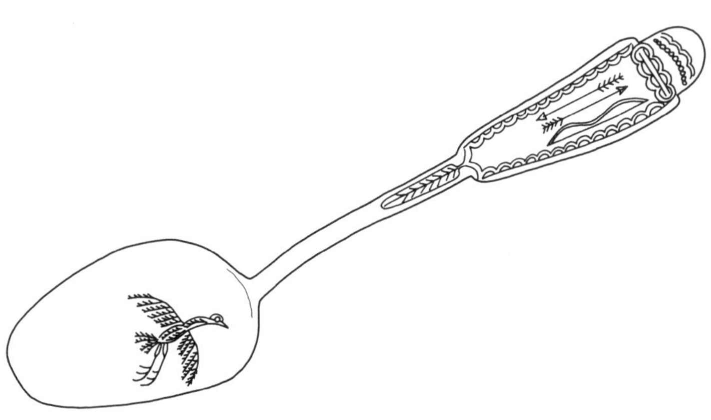

Indian spoon made in this century — a primitive piece of great charm.

ORIENTAL RUGS

Early in the eighteenth century the well-to-do American colonist was frequently the proud possessor of a "Turkey carpitt", although at first this exquisite and exotic object was usually to be found on a table rather than on the floor. Since that time the rugs and carpets of the Near and Middle East have been in and out of fashion as household effects. Twenty-five years ago oriental rugs could be bought in the Midwest for almost nothing. This is no longer true; now they are considered not only desirable, but very fashinoable, and consequently they are quite expensive. Another reason the prices of oriental rugs have increased recently is that many rugs are being purchased here and sent abroad to Europe and Iran, where they are valued more highly than in America and therefore fetch better prices.

Self-education and knowledgeable dealers of integrity are imperatives if you want to buy oriental rugs. Most "antique" orientals now offered for sale were made in the second half of the nineteenth century or the early twentieth century. Because of their greater availability, most collectors today are interested in the tribal or village rugs of this period. These rugs are not always easy to date and age is frequently not a prime consideration for collectors. Prices are usually based on the quality of the rug, on the rarity of the type, and, perhaps most important, on the condition of the rug, since severe wear makes a rug less attractive to many people and also limits the uses to which it can be put.

How can you determine quality? Only by careful study. It is particularly important to do as much reading and looking as possible. Two subjects which frequently confuse novice purchasers are the tightness of weave and the types of dye used. A tightly woven rug usually will wear better in floor use, but fineness of weave is not in itself an indication of quality. Certain tribal rugs were always coarsely knotted and that does not make them any less sought after, especially if the wool is of good quality. The colors in a rug are an important consideration in buying. Aniline dyes, which were gradually introduced into rug weaving in the last third of the nineteenth century, are not generally as attractive as natural dyes. Some of the early aniline dyes bled when washed, or disappeared completely. Many good, older rugs have both synthetic and natural dyes. Synthetic dyes detract from a rug's quality only to the extent that their use is aesthetically displeasing.

Before you buy a rug you should know how you wish to use it. If it is intended for floor use, any badly worn pile should be restored, unless you will be placing it where it will receive little wear. Remember that children, pets and high heels can be hard on any rug. Many collectors are hanging their orientals, especially the better pieces, not just because they are too valuable to wear out in floor use, but because they make extremely handsome wall decorations. When hanging rugs, consult a dealer or other expert about what method is most appropriate. When rugs need cleaning, send them only to reliable cleaners who are experienced in the handling of orientals.

BRASS AND COPPER

In many parts of the world in the last hundred years, brass and copper continued to be made into attractive kitchen utensils as well as into objects which were largely decorative. Sometimes you can determine the country of origin by the shape or decoration, but very often this is not possible. In particular, cooking utensils from a given period seemed to be made in much the same way in many countries. Brass and copper, even of the collectible period, is often expensive. Some of the items listed below, which represent a sampling of what is available, are rather expensive; others are more reasonably priced.

A pair of copper measures, ⅛ and ¼ pint. Made in the second half of the nineteenth century, exact time and place unknown.

Brass	*Copper*
Candlesticks	Saucepans
Candlesnuffers	Tea kettles
Ink wells	Dippers — strainers
Letter openers	Chestnut roasters
Mortar and pestles	Colanders
Paper clips	Funnels
Rulers	Ale warmers (British)
Telescopes	Spitoons
Curtain tie-backs	Apple butter kettles
Door knockers	Coffee pots
Book ends	Umbrella stands

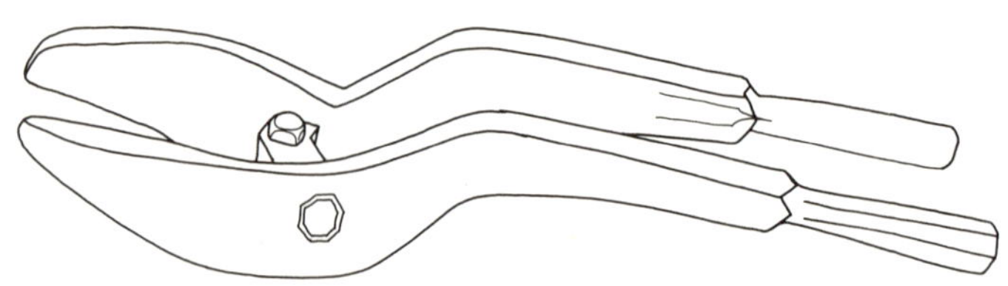

American wrought iron shoe stretcher, nineteenth century.

CAST IRON AND PLAIN TIN

Listed below are a variety of objects from the period of collectibles which make excellent decorations and which usually are not expensive. Much of the cast iron has been reproduced; this applies to the tin to a lesser degree. Buy for the attractiveness or usefulness of the object (my friends *use* their muffin tins and apple peelers!) and don't pay too much. Prices of these objects frequently vary, so do some comparison shopping first.

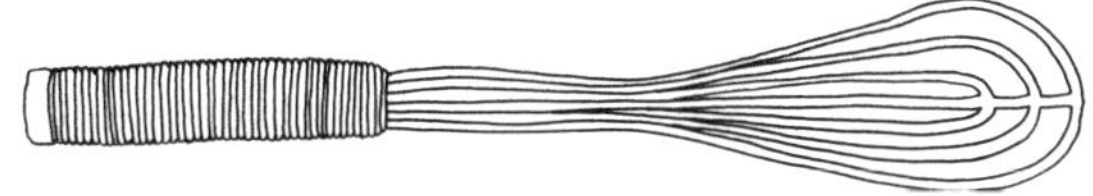

Tin whisk.

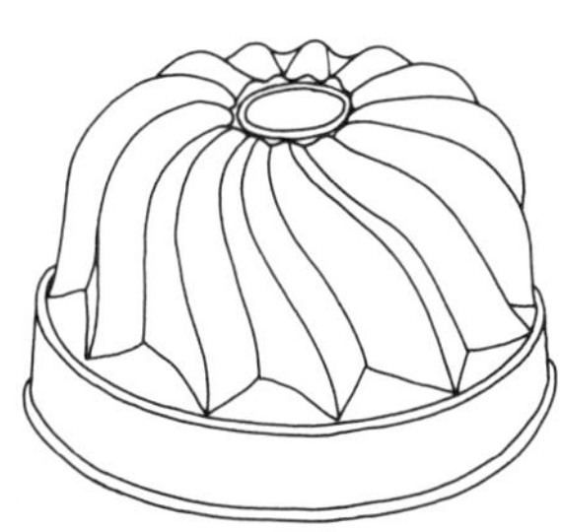

Tin pudding or cake mold.

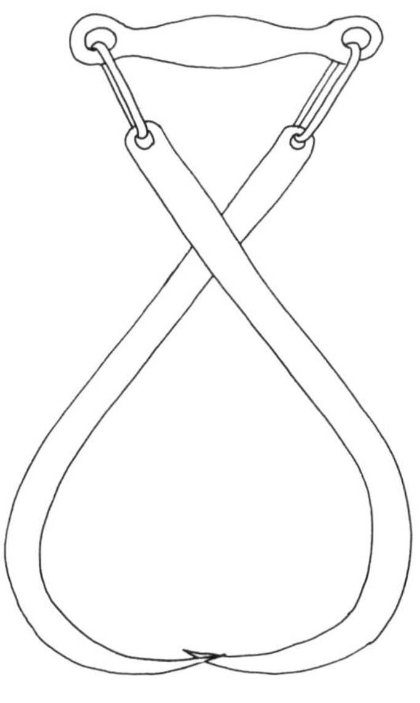

Cast iron ice tongs.

Cast Iron	*Unpainted Tin*
Trivets	Candle molds — many sizes
Boot jacks	Pudding molds
Penny banks	Cookie and chocolate molds
Sad irons	Tea caddies
Kettles	Tea dippers
Mailboxes	Cookie cutters
Apple peelers	Cake pans
Ladles	Spice boxes in sets
Match holders	Measures
String holders	Tea strainers
Waffle irons	Round bathtubs
Muffin pans	Match holders
Tea kettles	Candy boxes

Tin funnel with measuring indentations.

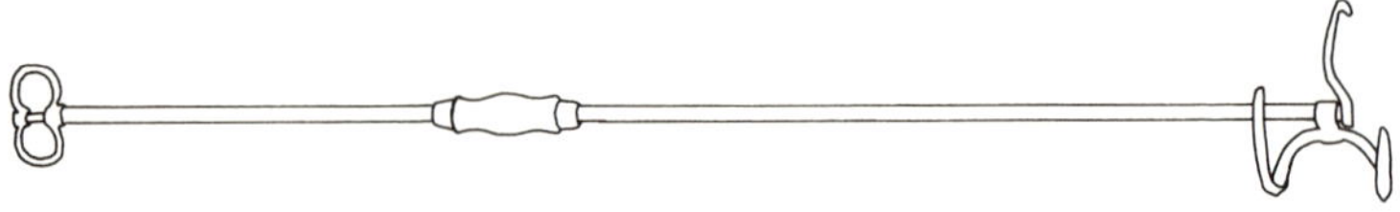

Iron and wood device used in stores to lift cans and small boxes from high shelves.

5

You and the Antique Dealer

Now that you have a general idea of what categories of antiques and collectibles exist, and of the special conditions in the Midwest, we can consider the problems of acquisition. Although there are numerous ways to buy antiques, and these will be examined in later chapters, the most important source for most collectors, and especially for beginners, will be the dealer. In order to understand why the dealer is so important in the distribution of antiques and collectibles, it is helpful to know something of the history of early collecting, as well as to understand the complexities of the current market situation.

Early Collectors and Dealers

Widespread interest in antiques is a relatively new phenomenon, rare even as recently as the late nineteenth and early twentieth centuries. For the most part, antiques were seen simply as "old stuff" of little value. Their aesthetic and cultural values were appreciated only by a small minority, whose collecting activities seemed so strange that they were ridiculed in contemporary newspaper cartoons as scroungers in trash cans.

Nonetheless the first American collectors included men

from the very top of society, such as James Pierpont Morgan, Henry Frick, John D. Rockefeller, Jr. and so on. Initially their interest was restricted to European antiques, which they bought through top dealers and auction houses of London and Paris in competition with their European counterparts.

Only somewhat later did their interest turn to American antiques, about which relatively little was then known. They were joined in this interest by a handful of affluent, middle-class Americans and lower on the social scale, by the first antique scouts, or "pickers", as we call them today. These pickers made forays into the countryside, knocking at back doors in a search for pieces mostly to sell to the few dealers and collectors existing then, and occasionally to keep for themselves. Isreal Sack, one of the greatest of the early dealers in American antiques, describes their operations admirably in the foreward to *Fine Points of American Furniture: Early American,* by his son Albert Sack.[10]

Wealthy or not, these early collectors had only their good taste to rely on. The wide range of books and journals on antiques, and the fine collections in museums did not then exist. Rather, the extensive research of the last fifty years which has led to both the publications and the museum collections is largely an outgrowth of their pioneering efforts. But precisely because there was so little general knowledge and demand, the early collectors could pick from an abundance of choice antiques and buy at their leisure. In such an environment, buying directly from the original owner of the merchandise was not only profitable; it was often necessary.

The Antiques Market Today

The situation today is quite different. The types of antiques acquired by the early collectors are now largely unobtainable

— many are displayed in museums, and those that do come on the market are quite beyond the means of most collectors. The pickers continue to ply their trade today, but there is less and less to be found in this way. Most of the more desirable antiques and collectibles have already been "discovered", and come on the market only when their owners, collectors themselves who have some idea of their worth, decide to dispose of them.

These changed circumstances have implications for both the dealer and the collector. From the standpoint of the private collector it is increasingly difficult and timeconsuming, especially in the Midwest, to buy without going through the intermediary of dealers. Because the Midwest was settled later, fewer antiques originated here than in the eastern United States. For this reason it has never provided as many opportunities for direct buying as in the East. Though many desirable antiques and collectibles now exist in the Midwest, many of them have been brought here, either by families that moved west, or more recently, by collectors and dealers who live here. When these people decide to sell, they frequently prefer to do so through a dealer because they want to avoid the time and trouble of advertising, waiting for a buyer (which as any dealer can tell you often takes a long time), and having to invite strangers into their homes. So it is not surprising that many of the better things here as elsewhere can be found most easily in the shops of competent dealers. You will have to pay more than if you bought directly, but you will not have to worry about repairing and restoring the items you buy. Moreover, many dealers will offer the advantages of a guarantee of authenticity and the privileges of return and exchange which are especially useful to new collectors. It is wise of course to make sure you understand exactly what a dealer's return policy is before buying.

Collecting Antiques in the Midwest

The Antiques Business

Let us next discuss the position of the dealer. The antiques business has always been different from most types of merchandising in that a) there are no dependable sources of supply where items in demand can be ordered, b) there are no uniform prices in buying and selling, and c) what is in demand in one part of the country may be sold somewhere else only after years of waiting. In these inflationary times the dealer's costs of placing his stock on the market have soared, whether he sells through a shop with all the usual overhead expenses, at home through advertising, through exhibiting at shows, or, as often is the case, through a combination of these.

Many people not knowledgeable about the trade are dismayed at the high markup on antiques. They are not aware that in addition to the problems of obtaining stock, the low turnover of antiques contributes greatly to the dealer's costs. Unlike the stock in your local supermarket, which is usually sold even before the market's bills come in, each antique is a unique item which must sit until someone who is looking for just that right object sees and buys it.

Dealers who see in the increased interest in antiques a chance to make money quickly learn that dealing in antiques is not the easy road to riches. On the contrary, it is an occupation which often demands hard physical labor, as well as long hours, high overhead and real dedication, usually for low monetary returns. In the long run the dealers who survive are not those looking for easy money, but rather those who are attracted by the beauty and historical significance of fine objects from the past, and who have chosen dealing in them as a way to provide themselves continuous contact with these treasures and with the people who appreciate them.

Of course there are scoundrels in the trade, dealers who knowingly will sell reproductions as the real article, or who "make" their own "antiques". But for collectors who know anything at all, they do not constitute much of a problem. It is not difficult to detect the "scoundrels", because they have, so to speak, a rather peculiar odor; other dealers (and there is a very genuine fraternity among good dealers) detest them, and this is rather obvious. A much more serious problem is dealers who are honest but lack sufficient knowledge. Because of the greatly increased interest in antiques there are many more of them about, and they can be quite dangerous precisely because they are so innocent. Very much like inexperienced collectors, they rely on the knowledge of others rather than their own, and sometimes with disasterous results. They are the dealers you must worry about, far more than the scoundrels.

How can you recognize the dealer who is both knowledgeable and honest? It should be clear from the above that the length of time a dealer has been in the trade is one indication, though by no means an absolute guarantee of quality. You can also tell a great deal from the condition of the dealer's merchandise. Dirt, dinginess, and tarnish have long since gone out of fashion; and trying to make antiques resemble reproductions of themselves by overpolishing is the mark of an inept dealer, or worse. Each piece at a good shop or show will be clearly described and priced, and the organization of the merchandise will reveal the professionalism and orderly habits of the competent dealer.

Finally — and most importantly — there is the dealer himself. If you have followed the advice given in the previous chapters, you will have a clear idea of what interests you and will know something of its history and attributes. Every experienced dealer knows the futility and irritation of starting from scratch in educating a buyer; but a good question or two will gain his attention and respect, and his answers soon will tell you whether or not he knows his business. If you are not satisfied, go elsewhere.

To acquire that crucial first good piece in the area you have chosen, it is probably wise to buy from a specialist dealer. His selection will be broad, his information will be more complete, and his reputation will be at stake when he dates and describes his merchandise. You are not going to make a spectacular buy from a specialist, since he will have a very clear idea of the market value of his goods. But you will get what you pay for, and in fact, the specialist dealer's price on a given item may well be the lowest available because he will have developed connections, in his area of concentration, which permit him to buy more advantageously than the non-specialist can.

When you find a fine piece in your area of interest, and are satisfied with the dealer, buy it. Ask that a description of what is known about the piece be written on the bill of sale so that you will have a record for insurance purposes and a reference if you later decide to sell. This description constitutes the dealer's guarantee as to the authenticity of what he has sold you, and you will also want it for protection in case you later find that he is mistaken. Of course, you must recognize that the description that can be provided will of necessity vary in its completeness according to the type of item purchased. English silver, for example, is usually very well marked; but depending on the period English ceramics often lack marks or other characteristics that make possible an attribution to a particular maker. Also, as a matter of pure practicality, it is unreasonable to ask for a detailed description of an article selling for only a few dollars.

Once you have bought that first really fine item, take it home and study it, handle it, live with it. You will be astonished to discover how much a deep familiarity with a good antique can sharpen your sense of quality in similar, and even in quite dissimiliar, objects.

Having carefully laid the cornerstone of your collection, you will begin to have the confidence to buy from non-specialist dealers, and from dealers who do not meet the high standards which we have described. It is from such dealers that you will be most likely to make really good buys. Let me explain why this is the case. Antiques are often bought in lots which include pieces of widely different quality and type. Since no single dealer can hope to be expert in all fields, some pieces from any lot will have to be set aside until such time as the dealer can research them; or else they will be put up for sale, often at low prices, with no claims made as to their attribution. It is merchandise in this "as is" category that gives the well informed collector the chance to make really good buys. In a sense the contest between buyer and seller is heavily weighted in favor of the buyer; the dealer, ideally, must be expert in many areas; the collector need only be expert in one.

I do not by any means, however, wish to leave the reader with the impression that the relation between collector and dealer ought to be one of antagonism. As a dealer I did not begrudge my customers inadvertent bargains; such transactions gave me an opportunity to expand my own knowledge, and they often resulted in long term relationships that satisfied all concerned. It is only the dealer who is under the mistaken impression that he knows everything who will feel cheated when he underestimates the value of an unfamiliar piece.

Indeed — and I cannot emphasize this point too strongly — a friendly relation with a well-informed dealer is by far the most valuable resource for any collector, no matter how experienced or knowledgeable. Here is what John W. Keefe, the curator of European decorative arts at the Art Institute of Chicago, has to say on the subject:

> Any serious collector should become acquainted with the dealers in his area, for one can learn more in an hour's discussion with a well-informed dealer than in twenty

hours of reading. I have a firm belief in the value of seeing and *handling* as many objects as possible, and obviously one can do this best through the agency of a friendly dealer.

The key to satisfactory relations with dealers, and, in fact, the key to successful collecting in general, is solid information in some category of antiques, no matter how narrow. There is simply no substitute for those first intelligent questions. He after all has constantly to contend with such questions as "what's that?" and "why does it cost so much?" — questions which reveal that the questioner knows little or nothing and cares less about the dealer's merchandise, which probably was difficult and costly to obtain. Once you have established your credentials as a serious collector, any good dealer will be glad to discuss related topics about which you know less. Such discussions will be invaluable to you, and will in themselves constitute a large part of the pleasure of collecting.

The Marketplace

Shows — Many people are familiar with antique shops, but shows are often overlooked as sources for buying. Shows, which are usually sponsored by a charitable organization but which are also occasionally managed by independent entrepreneurs, bring together in a single place a number of dealers on a periodic basis, usually once or twice a year. These shows are generally held in the same place each year, with each show running from two to five days; usually they open late each morning of the show and continue until rather late in the evening. Shows vary greatly in size; there may be anywhere from about 20 to 150 dealers exhibiting. Many of these shows have existed for years, and have built up a following of enthusiastic collectors who see them as festive occasions for buying and browsing. For the admission price of a few dollars you can see assembled all in one place a wide variety of antiques and collectibles.

At a good show you might see Queen Anne tables and a highboy or two, gaze at colorful arrays of Chinese export ware and displays of blue and white soft paste porcelain against dark English mahogany. You could pause to admire a whole Welsh cupboard full of softly gleaming pewter, or enjoy colorful and artfully draped quilts decorating booths full of painted country furniture. Looking more closely, you might see all sorts of treasures: an early blown decanter, a set of coin silver spoons, an old wooden scoop. Perhaps you will only admire the highboy which is selling for $15,000, but you might decide to buy the $10 coin silver teaspoon. Most dealers make a conscious effort to bring along to shows moderately priced merchandise as well as more exalted items; they know perfectly well that not everyone is able or willing to buy the more expensive things.

In Part II of this book, we have listed most of the prominent shows which exhibit in the Midwest; you will find these shows invaluable both for learning about antiques and collectibles, and for buying. Do not be intimidated or put off by the fact that some of these shows include very high priced merchandise. You want to see the best that is available, and this can be done most easily at good shows. When you actually start collecting you may find that shows are the best and sometimes the only sources for obtaining the items that you want. For a variety of reasons many dealers are closing their shops, and confining their selling activities to shows. If, for example, you are interested in American furniture in the styles of the eighteenth century, you will find that many of the best dealers do virtually all their selling at shows.

When you start attending shows you will discover that they vary greatly in the types of items displayed as well as in quality. Some shows are quite comprehensive in their offerings; others exhibit only antiques; still others have little but late collectibles. Some shows emphasize furniture, often both English and American, with only a small sampling of "decorative accessories", while others have mainly small antiques

What to Remember at Shops and Shows

• **If you have shopping bags or parcels, ask the dealer where you may place them out of the way. Dealers are increasingly worried about theft, and you will be less likely to break something if you are unencumbered.**

• **If there is an object which you wish to pick up or handle, ask the dealer if you may do so.**

• **If you are given permission to handle a small object, hold it over the counter or shelf on which it was displayed. If the object has come out of a cupboard, ask where it can be safely examined.**

• **Say how much you admire the things you are subjecting to examination, and leave objects which do not interest you alone. A dealer, like everyone else, likes to be told he is doing a good job.**

• **If there are no other customers needing attention, ask the dealer such questions as can help you round out your own knowledge. A very good way to do this is to examine a number of objects of similar type, and then ask the dealer if the price differences are due to variations in quality, condition, maker, or whatever.**

• **Remember that the dealer is a merchant. The good ones are also lovers of antiques, and are happy to talk about them if properly approached. But like any business man, primarily he is trying to make a living.**

and collectibles such as ceramics, glass and jewelry. There are a few shows which have only one category, such as glass or toys. Go to the shows, and look at and consider as much of what is available as you can. Then when the periods as well as the objects of your choice become firm in your mind, you will have sorted out which shows are the most useful to you given your interests, and you won't want to waste much time on the others.

You should keep in mind that shows place a great strain on the participating dealers, especially those who deal in

What to Forget at Shops and Shows

Forget to mention what antiques and collectibles your grandmother had.

Omit mention of the many treasures your family sent to the dump.

Neglect to give the dealer the story of the splendid things you bought, some time ago, for much lower prices than he is charging for the same articles.

Keep your own inventory of antiques to yourself, unless you are offering to sell them to him, or unless he needs this information to discover your special interests.

Never ask a dealer what he paid for an antique, or where he buys them.

Resist the temptation to ask the dealer for appraisals unless you are willing to pay for this professional service. Forget to ask dealers in English furniture about American furniture, or folk art dealers about silver. The antiques field is much too broad for one person to be an expert in everything.

quantities of fragile objects. Getting everything ready to pack, packing, loading, driving several hundred miles or more, unloading, getting electrical arrangements in order, getting the tables set up and draped, unpacking and arranging, and after the show the teardown, which is the same process in reverse, are so exhausting that there are few dealers who are not rather tired even at the start of a show.

If you intend only to look, by all means go to a show *on the second day;* it will be much less crowded and your viewing will be easier. There is often a lull in attendance late in the afternoon, which frequently is a good time for talking with a dealer as well as looking. Nonetheless, be careful not to get in the way of someone who seems to be doing the sort of looking that usually precedes buying. The dealer has gone to all the trouble and expense of exhibiting in order to sell; you should not hinder his efforts.

A very good show is high on the list of a collector's satisfactions and is looked forward to with great excitement. Here many choice antiques and collectibles can be seen all in one place. Often there is an opportunity, otherwise usually rare, to compare somewhat similar items for quality and price. There are few circumstances more rewarding to a collector than to go to a show the first day, find and buy what he wants, and if it is a big and splendid show such as one of Jean Crutcher's in Indianapolis, to go back the second day for that slower-paced looking that permits seeing many things of interest, which were precluded by the concentration necessary to the process of buying.

Shops — Now that shows have become established as such a valuable source for buying, shops have become, relatively speaking, somewhat less important for many collectors. Nonetheless, there are many excellent shops both large and small that are well worth exploring. There still are many dealers who never exhibit at shows, and the only way you will see their merchandise is to visit their shops. Also to be considered is that buying and selling at shops is much less harried than at shows. The beginning collector in particular may appreciate the greater leisure available for making decisions about buying. Certain categories which are especially difficult and time consuming to buy, such as oriental rugs, are probably best bought through shops unless you are very experienced in their handling.

Like the shows, shops vary greatly in size and quality. Many of the larger shops which have regular hours specialize in imported antique furniture, usually British, and compatible decorative accessories. Some of these shops have quite elegant and expensive merchandise. Again, do not be intimidated. You can learn much from looking at their quality merchandise, and you may be pleasantly surprised to find that they also have some less expensive, smaller items for sale.

The vast majority of antique shops, however, are rather small, and frequently are run by a single proprietor. These shops may specialize in a single category, such as quilts or golden oak furniture, or they may have what is called "a general line" of antiques: that is, an assortment of furniture, ceramics, glass and other items. As with the shows, they may have only late collectibles, or they may have very early and choice antiques.

These smaller antique shops are often forced to have somewhat irregular hours because their owners are so busy; often they are out on the road scouting for merchandise, or are away exhibiting at shows. Or perhaps they simply are busy putting into order and good repair the stock they plan to sell. Many of these dealers have a very small operation and they cannot afford to hire the full-time sales people which would be necessary to maintain regular hours. Also, selling antiques is a very personal business and many collectors want to talk to the dealer himself rather than to an assortment of hired help. For all these reasons, many of these shops operate "by chance or appointment"; some of them are simply an extension of the dealer's home. If you wish to visit one of these shops by all means call ahead, or you may find no one there. Also, if the dealer sells from his home, you cannot expect him to welcome an unannounced stranger.

It is the nature of small businesses to be ephemeral. Small antique shops in particular have a propensity for going out of business or changing rather drastically the nature of their operations. This is one of the reasons it would be impractical to try to list all of the thousands of antique shops that currently exist in the Midwest. Though our listing of shops cannot be as complete as our listing of good shows, we have tried to give as full and representative a listing as is possible of the best shops in the Midwest. Whenever possible, we have tried to cover all the specialities of interest to collectors, from early Chinese porcelain to late political memorabilia.

Many collectors will continue, doubtless, to prefer to do most of their buying at shops, and probably most of us enjoy spending a leisurely Saturday afternoon "antique hunting" in nearby neighborhoods. Many people on vacation find visiting new shops a pleasant recreation which makes travel more interesting. Our listing of shops presented in Part II will make such trips more productive. But particularly if you will be driving far, it is wise to phone ahead to check shop hours.

As you learn about antiques and collectibles, you will probably go through the same sorting out procedures with shops as for shows, and the same rules for gaining the co-operation of the dealer apply. Once you find dealers you like and respect and who have the merchandise you want, you may return often to see what they have for you. Of course you may discover some of your favorite dealers through shows and then continue to patronize them by visiting their shops or by corresponding with them about your desires. Many dealers are more than willing to search out merchandise for their customers. If a dealer you trust is familiar with your tastes and preferences, he may well be able to find you unusual pieces that you might never otherwise obtain. Needless to say this arrangement is a very good one for the collector as well as the dealer, and is one of the many reasons for seeking out a good relationship with the right dealer.

English "Chippendale" reverse curve tin-coated iron tray, japanned in a shrub, bird, flower, and foliage design similar to Chinese wall papers, hand painted for export in the second half of the eighteenth century. "Chippendale" as applied to these trays, made in the first half of the nineteenth century, is a misnomer; how it became attached to these objects is not known. Dimensions of this example 26¼″ x 31¾″. Bought at auction in 1972 for $5; appraised in 1974 for $200.

6

Buying at Auction

Auctions are not for beginners. When you buy at auction it is your responsibility to determine the condition and authenticity of the goods presented for sale; moreover, prices are unpredictable and all sales are final. Nonetheless, once you have become familiar with antiques and their market prices, you will find that auctions can be an excellent source for buying. Moreover, it is often exciting as well as instructive to attend a good one.

Auctions resemble shops and shows in that some, such as Southby Parke Bernet in New York City, handle the finest art and antiques, while at the bottom of the scale there are auctions which have little or nothing worth buying — or worse, which are run by unscrupulous auctioneers. A dishonestly run auction may have shills bidding on all or most of the lots to force prices up. Though you should know what to look for, you probably will never be bothered by shills, for they usually operate only where the whole set-up, including the "antiques", is a fraud. Between these two extremes there are many well-run auction houses throughout the country, including the Midwest, that have excellent antiques and collectibles. In the Midwest your chances of getting what you want are enhanced by being at a distance from the East Coast concentration of money and expertise at the very top of the auction business.

Though auction houses, like shops, vary in the kind and quality of merchandise presented for sale, there is an important difference between the dealer and the auctioneer. The latter personally chooses very little of the merchandise that comes under his hammer. So unless it is a thoroughly departmentalized gallery, with experts in every major field, the auctioneer cannot be expected to know everything — no one else does — about all the items presented for sale. The function of the auctioneer is rather to catalog and describe these items as well as can be done in a short space of time, to display them so that they can be examined before the auction, and then to manage the bidding, a job which requires a great deal of skill and stamina.

Some auction houses own nothing that they sell. For example, all the offerings at Christie's and at Southeby's in London are consigned. Other auction houses may hold some auctions where everything is consigned and others where some lots are owned by the house. The question of ownership is important because it may influence the selling price. If, for example, $200 has been paid by the house for a chair which receives a high bid of $25, the house can be expected to buy it back. Although this detracts from the spirit of the chase that permeates auctions where everything goes to the highest bidder, it is easy to understand that the house is unwilling to give away its merchandise. Of course the consignor of goods for auction may use a similar procedure to protect himself against inadequate bidding, especially if the goods are particularly valuable.

Despite these occasional restrictions on buying, auction prices are on the average lower than retail prices, and because of the uncertainties involved in bidding, the savings can sometimes be quite substantial. In fact, the reason most collectors buy at auction is precisely because it provides an opportunity to buy below the market price.

Collectors also buy at auction in order to acquire hard-to-find objects that occasionally become available there. This latter reason usually applies only to a few people, because well-advertised rarities, which usually appear at the larger auction houses, are going to be contested for by an imposing assemblage of well-heeled collectors, representatives of museums, and dealers. Such sales, however, can be quite dramatic.

To illustrate: recently a set of five Chippendale side chairs was consigned to Southeby's in London by a man who had bought them many years ago at an English country auction. One of Southeby's experts found that these chairs had certain stylistic and structural characteristics inconsistent with English Chippendale chairs, and sent photographs of the chairs to Southeby Parke Bernet in New York. Mr. Ronald De Silva, then head of Parke Bernet's American furniture department, found that they did indeed match a famous "sample" chair made by the noted Philadelphia cabinet maker, Benjamin Randolph, a chair now on exhibit in the Winterthur Museum. After more testing to ensure their authenticity, the chairs were put up for auction on November 16, 1974 — the successful bidder being Israel Sack, Inc. The winning bid of $207,500 broke the record of a price paid for a set of chairs sold at auction anywhere in the world.

This saga illustrates the care and expertise that is exercised at the top of the auction business. It also suggests the advantages of knowing what you are looking at and what it is worth, even when the objects you are pursuing are somewhat less exalted. You will find that across the country well-run auction houses take a great deal of care to describe objects and multiple-piece lots correctly. Many of the smaller houses call in experts for consultation when necessary. Like a good dealer, a good auctioneer has a reputation to protect, and he is very careful of it.

How to Bid at Auction — Once you decide to start buying at auction houses, the first step is to familiarize yourself with their operations. Procedures differ at auction houses, so even if you have some experience, it is worth taking some time to find out just how the auction is run before bidding in an unfamiliar place. Always read with care the terms of sale. If there is no catalogue containing the terms of sale, listen to the announcement of these terms made by the auctioneer before the start of each session. An almost universal condition of sale is that everything is sold "as is". Although this may seem a contradiction to all the expertise that is expended on correct attribution at the top of the trade and all the descriptions in carefully compiled catalogues, this "as is" selling at auction is a tradition several thousand years old.

We have outlined below a series of steps to follow if you plan to buy at auction. If auctions are new to you, you may wish to attend a few sessions just to get a feel for the bidding before preparing yourself to bid.

1. Investigate the auction galleries near you and ask to be put on their mailing lists.

2. If you plan to attend an auction, go to the preview early and buy a catalogue if there is one.

3. Have with you a notebook and all the equipment necessary to examine carefully the objects that interest you. A magnifying glass will be useful for examining the marks on silver and ceramics as well as for scrutinizing glazes, finishes, and so forth. A small magnet will enable you to distinguish bronze from iron with a bronze finish. If you are interested in furniture, take along a measuring tape and flashlight (so you can examine the undersides of tables, case pieces and the like); if jewelry interests you, bring along a jeweler's loupe.

4. Survey quickly the lots that interest you before starting to go over them carefully and making your notes. If there are more lots than permit careful examination and accurate note taking, concentrate on the ones that are your first choice.

5. After careful examination and note-taking on condition, write down the price each lot is worth to you. Unless further research at home or in a museum or library gives you reason to change your mind, *don't go above your first estimate* of what you should pay, in spite of the excitement of the bidding. You can expect your opinions in these matters to change with experience, but while you are first learning about auction prices it is better to be cautious.

6. If some of the objects that interest you are in locked cases, ask to see them. You must examine each object closely. No experienced auction buyer ever bids on anything without a close examination. Occasionally it is proper to tip the attendants who open the cases.

7. Most auction houses use numbered bidding cards to identify the bidders. If cards are used, the back of your card is the best place to jot down the numbers of the lots you succeed in buying, as well as your winning bid. Otherwise use your notebook (or auction catalogue), which is also a good place to keep a record of what prices other objects brought at the session you are attending. *Keep this notebook.* It contains important information about antiques you have examined and what they sold for at auction at a particular time and place. For those items you buy, it can be a valuable reference in case something is damaged or missing from a lot. If you get a bidding card, keep it with you. You are responsible for its use in bidding.

8. It is essential to pay strict attention to the auctioneer — everything takes place very rapidly at an auction. Attentiveness is especially necessary when lots with more than one object are up for sale. Sometimes a pair of candlesticks is bid on at so much a stick, although they are sold as a lot. For example, the auctioneer may say: "This pair of candlesticks is being sold as a pair and bid at so much *each*". Or: "Lot 247, consisting of fifteen antique pattern glass goblets, slight chipping on three, is being bid at so much *each*." In the latter case, if the winning bid is $21, lot 247 costs its purchaser $315.

9. If the crowd is large, it is best to sit back of center, where you can see as much as possible of the audience as well as the auctioneer. You will soon know who the dealers are by their pattern of bidding. Dealers usually buy a much wider range of articles and in much greater quantity than would a collector.

10. Find out beforehand the conditions of sale regarding payment. Learn if checks are acceptable, and if so, what kind. This can avoid considerable embarrassment later.

11. Get receipts for any deposits or payments, and keep them.

12. Pick up your purchases as soon as possible, especially the fragile items.

Many collectors and even some dealers new to the trade take an unsophisticated view of dealers buying at auctions, considering them to be their mortal enemies. Since dealers must buy most of their merchandise well below the retail price if they are to make a profit, they can only be of annoyance to one another, not to collectors. There are two exceptions to this rule: one in buying, and the other in selling. The first exception occurs when a dealer is bidding for a private collector. For this service, which involves examining and authenticating the object, as well as doing the bidding, the dealer usually gets ten per cent of the purchase price. Understandably, many beginning collectors consider this arrangement a bargain. In such instances, however, the dealer's bidding can indeed interfere with that of other collectors if the dealer's own client is willing to pay very well for the object.

The other circumstance in which the activities of dealers at auction can frustrate the interests of the collector is when the collector himself is the consignor of the goods put up for auction. Here, especially if the antiques are rare and choice, the consignor will want to protect them against unreasonably low bidding. He can do this by setting what is known as a "reserve price", below which he will not permit the object to be sold. Auctions are a gamble for the consignor because in many instances it is not possible to know if the collectors and dealers whose presence is necessary for reasonable bidding will be in attendance. The reserve price also safeguards the consignor's antiques from the operations of the "ring". The ring is a group of dealers who collaborate in order to keep auction prices down by having one of their number bid for all on certain objects. If there is little competition from collectors and other dealers and no reserve price, the ring can buy at ridiculously low prices. No remedy has been found for the unethical practices of the ring. Nonetheless, the only persons who can be consistently hurt by the ring are the consignor — hence the reserve price by which he can protect himself, and the auctioneer, who gets a fixed percentage of the selling price. But despite the occasional operation of rings, the hard fact is that the auction business would be in trouble without the consistent stabilizing effect of dealer participation, both in buying and in consigning items to be sold.

You can learn much from the way dealers bid. The antique business is a difficult one in which to become proficient, and a dealer who does not know what he is doing in an auction room is not likely to be in business long. If you discover a ring in operation at an auction, you have the assurance of several expert opinions regarding the desirability of the antiques for which they are bidding. If some of these are what you want, you should have little difficulty in getting them insofar as the ring is concerned. They will leave the bidding long before the bids approach retail prices.

When you first attend auctions you may be dismayed by the speed with which the bidding takes place, but this is the only way hundreds of lots can be sold in a day. You will be impressed by the adroit handling of many bidders by the auctioneer — this requires considerable expertise as well as insight into human psychology. If you are worn out at the end of an exciting session, just think of the auctioneer!

Although auction prices are usually lower than market prices, the price on any particular item depends on what dealers and collectors are present, and, of course, how they are bidding. Unpredictable things happen at auction. Occasionally you may buy a desirable antique for a fraction of its retail price, just as you might make a spectacular buy in a shop from a dealer who does not know its value; but do not depend on consistently finding incredible bargains. After all, we would not want to see our own carefully assembled collection sold for a very small part of its value. It is obvious that if these exceptions became the rule, the selling of antiques at auction would end. Nonetheless, it pays to keep your eyes open for the unusual opportunities that occasionally arise. I have myself made some remarkable auction purchases. How they were possible with several hundred people present has never been quite clear to me, but these happy occasions seem to be part of the Midwest antique scene.

Two Tiffany candle lamps, sold at auction in 1974. The one with the chimney brought $750; the other one $575. Photograph courtesy of C. P. Terry Dunning of Dunning's Auction Service, Elgin, Illinois.

Other Sources for Buying: House Sales, Garage Sales, Rummage Sales, Thrift Shops and Flea Markets

The increasing scarcity of antiques and worthwhile collectibles have made many of these hunting grounds much less fruitful than they have been in the past. Nonethless, if you have the time to spend, you may be able to find good things priced well below the market.

House Sales — You should be aware that sometimes house sales are bogus. Unless you know the people who own the merchandise or whose estate sale it is, you should scrutinize the setup rather carefully, because some of the offerings could be stolen goods. Or it might turn out that a dealer has set up a sale of his goods as if it were a private house sale, in which case his ownership of the merchandise may be legitimate, but probably the prices will be inflated. Prices at a house sale should be well below those in a shop, or you would not be interested, given that you must buy the merchandise in "as is" condition and make any needed repairs yourself, and that all sales are final, not to mention the other inconveniences of buying in this manner, such as setting forth at odd hours of the day and night, frequently very early in the morning, waiting in long lines, and sometimes not seeing a single thing you want after all your efforts.

Assuming the house sale you are attending is a legitimate one, the procedure to follow is very simple. Go to the sale *very early* with the following items: the equipment recommended for previewing auctions (that is, a small magnet, tapemeasure, flashlight, etc.) and one or two strong shopping bags with some padding to protect fragile objects.

At a house sale you cannot stand on ceremony. Move quickly, and when you see what you want pick it up and put it in your bag. Use one bag for the heavy, less breakable objects, the other one with the padding for more fragile items. If you find something that won't fit into a shopping bag take it to the check-out table and leave it there. If necessary pay for it right away, but be sure to get a receipt, and then go back to your hunting. After you have attended a few house sales you will get the hang of it; that is, if you don't decide you never want to see another one again. People are rarely indifferent in their attitudes toward house sales; they either delight in them or detest them.

Flea Markets — Flea markets vary enormously in quality. Those that are worthwhile, whose offerings are not just drugstore seconds, used automobile items and absolute trash, are often very much like antique shows and should be treated as such. Some flea markets in fact offer more antiques than many shows.

Thrift Sales, Garage Sales, and Rummage Sales — These sources for hunting are rather like house sales, but generally speaking, are still less worth your time. The same rules apply as for house sales: that is, go early and with the proper equipment.

Thrift Shops, Second-Hand Stores, etc — If these shops operate on a seasonable basis, as thrift shops in particular sometimes do, go early in the season. As with these other sources for bargain hunting listed above, make sure you are sufficiently knowledgeable to know what is a bargain. You will feel very foolish indeed if you discover that after spending a couple hours prowling around a dusty junk store or dirty garage for your "treasure", you could have bought it all scrubbed and clean, for the same price at the antique shop down the road. Whatever sector of the marketplace you are exploring, be it ever so humble, you need to know what you are buying, and what the prices are.

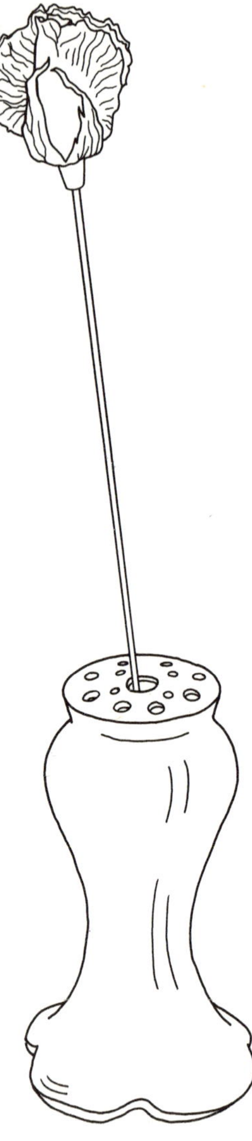

Art nouveau gilded metal and green enamel hat pin, circa 1885–1910.

7

Last Words of Advice:
Suggestions and Cautions

In ending this section of our book, I would like to offer a few final words of advice. These ideas may not be shared by everyone in the field, but they have been formed by years of personal experience both as a dealer and as a collector. One consideration in making decisions about collecting is the role played by fashions in the antiques market. In the history of collecting, fashions have come and gone. Some antiques which were once highly fashionable are not so now simply because they are no longer available on the market for collecting. It is now impossible, for example, to collect sets of fifteenth and sixteenth century tapestries; it is virtually impossible to buy French palace furniture and the more elegant versions of French silver and soft paste porcelain.

Many other antiques and collectibles have remained available but are not always in public favor. Certain categories and styles have at times been considered highly desirable, but at other times have remained neglected for shorter or longer periods of time. One example is the American quilt. A few years ago only museums and a handful of collectors were interested in fine quilts; most people interested in antiques would not consider buying them for anything approximating what is currently considered their true value. This was all the more remarkable considering that it does not take arcane knowledge to assess the merits of a quilt. Other examples of objects, most of them not antiques, which were once ignored but which are now considered highly desirable are oriental rugs, American Indian arts and crafts, art glass, and just about everything made under the direction of Louis Comfort Tiffany. Now that all these categories and many more are fashionable, their prices have risen substantially.

If your collecting tastes parallel current fashions, fashionable purchases may be just right for you. On the other hand, you may discover later that the promoted categories are not really what you wanted. If a fashionable category interests you, a good mental test is to ask yourself if you would still like these objects if they were no longer the latest word, appearing in all the home decorating magazines and shops and in the homes of your friends. Another question to ask yourself is whether the promoted object represents a level of craftsmanship and aesthetic worth commensurate with its price. Or is it something that is easily reproduced, even something that you could perhaps make yourself? If the object you like costs no more than would something made today using equivalent materials and requiring similar skills and labor, you can consider your purchase a safe one even if it can be reproduced or is very expensive.

Some objects, such as late bottles, Carnival, Heisey, or Depression glass, and the glass candy containers that were sold in quantity in railway depots and elsewhere can indeed be easily reproduced, and many of them are. The same can be said for most cast iron objects such as banks, whether mechanical or not. Many of these objects were originally made entirely by machine; in such cases there is no difficulty at all in making reproductions look as old as the originals.

You may think I am not serious in suggesting that you may be able yourself to make some of the things you would like to collect, but one category which lends itself admirably to such efforts is American folk art. Its current very high prices may encourage you even more to "do for yourself". The whole spirit of American folk art is that it is not beyond the reach of anyone who is interested and willing to try. Are we any less talented than the generations that recently preceded us? Of course not. Consider all those plain, but nicely dovetailed, pine boxes of various sizes waiting in antique shops for someone to decorate them. There is wood to be carved, embroideries to be made, tin to be painted. You will find much to inspire you in the books on American folk art, as well as in modern exhibits at galleries and museums, whether you prefer to follow past traditions or to branch out into the future.

"Limited Edition" Merchandise — A highly promoted category of which you should be particularly wary are the many "limited edition" objects which are so touted for their investment possibilities. Limited editions had an honorable beginning several generations ago when two highly respected Danish ceramic firms, Royal Copenhagen and Bing and Grondahl, issued a plate for each Christmas. These plates were made in distinctive blues, dated, and after each year's run the molds were destroyed. Numerous people in the United States enjoyed collecting these plates, and because of their attractiveness and relative rarity they remained in demand and increased in value as the years went by.

But for more than ten years now the market has been flooded with objects of every description, made in a whole host of materials, which are characterized as limited edition collectibles: plates, bells, plaques, mugs, ingots, figurines, jewelry, and so on. Though the number in the edition is seldom specified, they are all represented as investments. The effect of this flood of "limited editions" on the respected Danish Christmas plate series has been a classic example of the economic principle of "bad money driving out the good". After years of steadily increasing in value, these plates have now depreciated so sharply that they are difficult to sell. Before "investing" in any of these "limited editions", you would do well to consider the present fate of the Danish Christmas plates. Among all the vast quantities of this "limited edition, investment" merchandise there probably are a few objects that will remain limited and that have enough intrinsic worth that they may eventually increase in value. However, the wisdom of trying to sort out this conglomeration is very dubious. If you like some of these objects, it is best simply to buy them as the gift shop merchandise which they are.

Some Neglected Categories — The antique or collectible which is out of fashion is frequently neglected, simply because there is little information available on the subject. However, the publication of good books, especially those that result from major exhibitions, can often be counted upon to stimulate the interest of collectors, and then eventually to elevate prices. Examples of categories which are currently neglected, I feel unjustly, are American Empire furniture and various British ceramics such as lustre, gaudy Welsh, and some ironstones. These categories can usually be had in today's market at reasonable prices, and are worth your consideration.

Taken as a whole, American Empire furniture lacks the aesthetic qualities of the earlier styles. Nonetheless, this furniture was as well crafted, and made out of woods as luxurious, as the more sought-after furniture made immediately before it. Very few people today are furnishing rooms all from one period, and there are excellent Empire pieces that not only get along very well with other styles, but also lend a touch of the flamboyant that can make a room very exciting.

American Empire cherry chest with tiger maple veneered drawer fronts and shallow half-round moldings around top. The glass nobs are original — these rather plain octagonal nobs were made at the Sandwich glass factory and elsewhere. Circa 1825–30. $75 paid; appraised for $750.

There are also more restrained chests of drawers, tables, sideboards and other such pieces that are quite attractive and well worth consideration.

Lustre, in its many lovely forms and colors, is a classic example of a category which has languished in comparative neglect because of the lack of readily available information. The exceptions that have increased in price are pieces of unusual aesthetic or historical interest. There is only one comprehensive book written on the subject: *Old English Lustre Pottery,* by W. D. John and Warren Baker (Dr. Baker was a professor at Northwestern University, and a major collector of lustre). This book was published in 1951 in an edition of 1000 copies and reissued in 1962 in another edition of the same size. Understandably it is difficult to buy, but museums with art departments usually have it available for reference. There is also available one small book which is excellent. (See the bibliography.)

English lustre is an unique decoration made by fusing a thin layer of metal on a ceramic base. Lustre ceramics include a wide variety of decorative techniques such as "resist": in this technique the design is painted in a resistant material and the object fired after being covered with the metal. Later it is washed, and then the pattern appears. Transfer printing and freehand painting are also used. An object is classified as lustre whether it has but a single banding of lustre decoration or whether the entire object is covered with metal. Some tea sets, for example, were covered with platinum in imitation of more expensive silver sets. Except for rare pieces, the prices of lustre are much lower than those of other ceramics of the same period which are of comparable workmanship and aesthetic value. It is not difficult to learn how to tell old from new lustre; with a piece or two in your possession and the usual careful looking you should have no trouble.

158

This early lustre banded jug has several interesting features. This coach-and-four transfer print is one used for a number of dated pieces for at least fifteen years. Nonetheless, coaching jugs are scarce; the transfer is black, overprinted in black, yellow, red, and blue. The neck and the reverse side are hand painted in floral designs. The jug is made of a white soft-paste porcelain of a glassy translucence. And it is a presentation piece to Mary Wain, 1825.
Photograph by Noel Kopald

There are other types of British ceramics which are also attractive but which usually sell well below other ceramics of the same period. One example is gaudy Welsh, an English bone china with Imari-type decorations, made from about 1830 to 1845. (Some gaudy Welsh was made later but with a piece of the earlier period in your possession you should have little difficulty in telling the later objects from those made earlier.) Another good buy is gaudy ironstone. It shares the same Imari-type color palette, that is, dark blues, reds and rusts) as gaudy Welsh, but the decorative style is still more removed from classic Imari decoration. To the best of my knowledge there are no books that both list and illustrate all the patterns in which they were made. Another British ironstone worth your consideration is the transfer-printed ironstone made from about 1840 to 1850. This attractive and inexpensive ware is printed in pastels and pale blues, but looks very different from the earlier transfer printed earthernwares described below.

If you are one of the many who love blue and white ceramics but cannot afford the more fashionable types, you might consider English blue and white transfer-printed creamware of the 1810 to 1830 period which was *not* made for the American market. It is a delightful genre and much more reasonably priced than the much-sought-after Anglo-American historical china of the 1820–1830 period. The word "china" is used here in its generic sense; creamware is of course earthenware, not porcelain. If you do enjoy the historical associations of Anglo-American china, you might consider collecting the slightly later pastel pieces which were made from about 1830 to 1840; they are excellent Americana and less in demand. Interestingly, it was a display of pastel, transfer-printed earthenware, probably Anglo-American china, in a pine cupboard in Vermont in 1823 that aroused Henry Francis du Pont's interest in American antiques, the result of which is the Winterthur Museum, the single greatest col-

Bookplate circa 1915 in the style of Arthur Rackham. Bookplates are very collectible.

---

lection now available for our viewing. Although not cheap, these pastels tend to cost much less than the dark and medium blues made in the 1820s; collectors have been so obsessed in their devotion to the "old blue" that those who are interested in buying the pastels should have a fairly free field.

With a little digging you may be able to find a variety of objects that are similarly undervalued. For example, although original prints, maps and colored engravings have risen a good deal in price recently, they still offer good value for the money spent and are unusual decorative additions to any home. Glass collectors may be interested to know that certain early English glasswares, such as wines and rummers, are also well priced. And finally, you might consider European folk art as a low-cost alternative to its American counterpart. Not only is it quite attractive in its own right, but in it we can also see how it influenced our own folk art. (Mexican folk art is still less expensive, though quite different in style.)

CAUTIONS

What are some of the things to look out for in buying?

Reproductions — The first rule is to avoid being fooled by reproductions. You can do this not only by being familiar with what the old, genuine piece looks like, but also by familiarizing yourself with whatever reproductions are on the market. Most of these are made and sold quite honestly for what they are, but only a few of them, such as some Williamsburg reproductions, are clearly and indelibly marked as such. If they are taken from the gift shops where they are legitimately sold, then scuffed up a bit and relocated in an "antique" setting, they may easily pass for the real thing with those who are unwary.

Fakes — You also have to realize that some reproductions are made expressly to deceive, and that such fakes may always exist whenever there is sufficient financial incentive. Once you have decided what to collect, try to assess just how easy and how profitable it would be to reproduce such objects. Little more than common sense and some knowledge of the objects is needed for this evaluation.

As we have mentioned earlier, some items such as cast iron and certain types of glass can be reproduced very easily. Because cast iron and glass have the same characteristics now as they did when the objects being reproduced were originally made, if the same old molds are used or new molds made from original objects, the reproduction should look exactly like the original.

Other objects, such as early ceramics, are much more difficult to reproduce because the methods of production are so changed and the formulas used in the pastes and bodies varied so that it is impractical to try to duplicate them exactly. Still other objects are completely unsuited for faking; no one, at least yet, would want to wear himself out trying to fake an old quilt.

Most often the faker will either take shortcuts to save costs, which will make his copy inexact, or else the reproduction will differ from the original simply because of the faker's insufficient understanding of all the object's characteristics, as these were shaped in and by a very different period from that in which the faker is working. In either case, if you know what to look for in the originals, you will not be fooled. To illustrate, reproductions have been made of some of the very early soft paste porcelains which are now so expensive, but since they have almost always been made in the now-standard harder pastes, they will not deceive anyone who knows how to distinguish between hard and soft paste.

Furniture represents a special problem for the faker. In the first place, it is very costly to try to duplicate the skills of the old cabinet makers and very difficult, if not impossible in some cases, to find woods of the quality used in the past. Moreover, it is extremely difficult to fake convincingly the look of old wood and old paint. As wood ages, its color naturally mellows and acquires what is called a patina. Only time can create this patina, and it is desired by collectors not only because it constitutes a large part of the beauty of an antique, but also because its existence provides in large degree a guarantee of the authenticity of a piece. In particular, the unfinished soft woods generally used in the interior construction of American furniture acquire over time a color which cannot be faked. Similarly, old paint looks quite different from new, and has very different characteristics; it is hard, even brittle, whereas new paint is rather soft. Once a piece of furniture has lost its patina or old paint, it is easier to make changes on the piece that are not too noticeable.

As a result of these problems, fakes in furniture are rarely built from the ground up. What is easier, and therefore much more likely, is to "enrich" genuine pieces too plain for some tastes with carving or inlay, or, now that it is so fashionable, with paint. Pieces are sometimes "improved" by adding more elegant feet, or by scalloping the edges of aprons. Minor operations are also sometimes carried out on furniture to render it more salable, such as removing the wooden panels from cupboard doors and replacing them with glass.

Perhaps even more common than enriching pieces is to "marry" them; that is, to put together different tops and bottoms. This is a perfectly acceptable practice, which makes otherwise incomplete pieces available for use at a lower cost. But the customer should know if a piece is married, just as he should know all the repairs and restorations made on a piece.

As the supply of available old furniture continues to de-decrease, married pieces and furniture that has undergone major restoration will probably become more acceptable to many people as they are so much less expensive if sold for what they are, than entirely original furniture. There are many such pieces on the market, and when they are married or restored with some sensitivity to how the object should look, they can offer quite attractive low-cost alternatives for the collector on a budget.

Dating — Another question which concerns many collectors is the problem of dating. We would all like to believe that the objects we collect are as old as possible, and novice collectors in particular tend to attach an inordinate amount of importance to the question of exactly when an object was made rather than to the intrinsic qualities of the object itself.

In many categories, and especially with furniture, one of the chief aids to dating is style; but again, especially for furniture, style can be a misleading guidepost. Because of the difficulties of travel and the slowness of communications, American styles did not change rapidly outside major cities during either the colonial period or the early years of the republic. Styles which started in major urban centers at the very top of society filtered down slowly to those of lesser means, or to those living in more provincial areas; they also drifted slowly westward with the frontier. As a result, furniture continued to be made in certain styles long after it had first been introduced.

Moreover, to further complicate the question of dating, many eighteenth century furniture styles were made to order well into the nineteenth century with the same fine woods and excellent craftsmanship that had characterized the eighteenth century work. Some people obviously preferred the older styles and were able to order what they wanted — namely, replicas. Without precise historical documentation, which very little furniture has, there is no very satisfactory way to draw the line between the eighteenth and nineteenth century in these cases.

So what are you to think when you see at shops and shows so much furniture marked "American, eighteenth century"? Granted, most of these offerings are in the styles of the eighteenth century: usually they are elegant provincial or country versions of Queen Anne and Chippendale styles, or they are early American windsors. But given the small size of the American population in the eighteenth century — it is estimated to have been about 2,600,000 in 1774 — and given that only a certain percentage of this population could afford such furniture, it is difficult to believe that all such furniture which survived and has found its way to the market could actually have been made in the eighteenth century. This dating by style is not necessarily an attempt to deceive, however; it is just a consequence of the widespread homage we pay to the magic of dates, especially eighteenth century ones.

So where does all this leave us? It is the quality of design and construction that are important, not precise dates. Fine American antique furniture is very much worth having, even without a provenance — something which few of us can afford. In the bibliography you will find books that discuss all the things you need to look for in a piece of furniture, from the "good, better and best" versions of the styles to details of construction. Make notes of this advice and apply it to whatever type and style of furniture interests you. If you have done enough comparative shopping to have some knowledge of what price seems within reason for an object of its type and excellence, and if the piece satisfies you, buy it and enjoy it.

To a lesser extent, this approach can also be applied to silver. An out-of-period replica can be a very satisfactory object if it retains not only the style and materials but also the spirit of the period it represents. A replica is very different from the object usually referred to as a "revival" piece. The latter may borrow motifs from an earlier period, but the spirit of the rendition is so different that is has to be considered a different style.

Practical Considerations in Buying Furniture — Of all the antiques we collect, we are most likely to use antique furniture for the purposes for which it was originally intended. Few of us today would serve tea from an eighteenth century teapot or carve the Sunday roast on a Chinese export platter. But none of us would buy a chest of drawers, even an eighteenth century chest, without expecting to use it. Because of this expectation, you should take into consideration practical matters such as convenience of use and ease of maintenance as well as aesthetic appeal when buying.

Generally speaking, antique furniture is quite sturdy, especially when compared to modern furniture, and it is not difficult to keep in good order if you follow a few simple guidelines. Assuming that your furniture is in good repair and the finish in satisfactory condition when you buy it, the rules of maintenance are simple indeed: dust it regularly to keep it clean, treat it with reasonable care, and above all provide proper humidification. Low humidity is very hard on wood, and the shrinkage it causes can loosen joints and even cause cracking. Also, when glue dries out, joints and veneer will loosen. It is much easier to keep antique furniture looking attractive than modern furniture. One scratch on your Scandinavian teak dining table and it looks a mess, but a few dents and scratches on an antique are simply part of its unique, personal history; no one should expect or want an antique to look new. Keep in mind that water, alcohol and heat are hard on any finish. Do not set hot dishes directly on the wood, and use a good paste wax on tabletops to protect against accidental spills. Never, never use waxes containing silicone on any good furniture. One last pointer: keep your furniture out of direct sunlight.

The Perils of Chairs — Because of the heavy use they receive, chairs do require more attention to maintenance than do most other types of old furniture. Upholstered furniture in particular can be expensive to maintain in good order. The punishment of getting up and sitting down, especially on upholstered pieces, puts a constant strain not only on the webbing, springs, twine, burlap, and hand-sewn edges — in fact, on all the things that are unseen and so are not considered until they give way — but on the woodwork of the frame. The tacking rails will take only so much punishment before they have to be renewed. With the demise of the apprentice system in upholstery generations ago, the degenerating quality of factory-made furniture, and now the *coupe de grace* of efficient built-in obsolescence, we are all faced with problems of finding comfortable seating furniture without going broke. My husband Jens and I were in the furniture repair, restoration and upholstery business until 1969, and we saw how quality declined even while the costs for this sort of work climbed to almost unbelievable heights.

If you do buy antique upholstered furniture, keep in mind that each reupholstering will be very expensive, and that the frame of the piece can take only so much hammering. For this reason, when you are having a piece upholstered, try to select durable fabrics which will last as long as possible. There are many reproductions of antique fabrics on the market, but some are much better in quality than others. Some of the better upholstery lines have designed fabrics in styles appropriate for formal period furniture which looks quite delicate, but which in fact are quite sturdy. You may have to do some looking to find the right fabric and the services of a competent upholsterer, but you cannot hand over a fine old chair or sofa to just anyone.

There is no question that old chairs can be delightful, and there are a number of ways you can minimize your difficulties if you cannot resist their charms. If you can buy chairs with slip seats rather than with upholstery that goes over the frame, you can save yourself much trouble and expense. If you are at all handy you can probably repad and recover them yourself. When buying small occasional chairs, you might consider using them more as decorative accents for your home rather than as everyday seating furniture. Particularly if they are fragile, try to place them where they will not invite heavy use. If you do want chairs for daily use in the kitchen or dining room, it is wiser to stick to the sturdier plank-bottom types, especially when children are present.

And remember that tilting back in any chair, no matter how sturdily constructed, will quickly destroy it. If you must tilt, get yourself a rocking chair.

Furniture in the Rough — If you decide to save money by buying your furniture "in the rough", you must be able to do your own repair and restoration work; otherwise you may end up spending more money than if you had bought a similar item in ready-to-use condition. If you do plan to do your own work, remember that when in doubt it is better to do too little than too much. In particular, do not be too eager to "strip and refinish" old furniture. Furniture in old paint is now considered very desirable by perceptive collectors; if you remove this old paint you will decrease the value of your piece. If you do not happen to like the look of old paint, let someone else who does buy the piece. Whenever possible you should try to preserve the old finish and limit your efforts to protecting it; such an approach preserves the integrity of the piece as an antique, and you will find also that it is much less work.

When a piece of furniture has a clearly inappropriate, later finish, such as dime-store enamel on inlayed or veneered hardwoods, it must be removed. But be careful that you do not "skin" the piece, that is, remove the surface of the wood, because you will then remove any patina and tool marks which give old furniture its character. To avoid skinning, do not use any but the finest sandpapers for smoothing, and use them sparingly. If someone has put chainmarks or something else dreadful on the top of the table you just bought, you probably will not be able to disguise the scars, especially if they go across the grain, but if you take off the top layer of wood to remove them, keep in mind that you will then have an entirely "new" tabletop, and that it will take years and years for the old color of the wood to return. Alas, one of the sadder facts of life. Before you start any projects make sure you know what you are doing. Consult the books suggested in the bibliography, and when possible seek out the advice of those who both care about antiques and are knowledgeable about the restoration of furniture.

Antiques as an Investment — A last question that often concerns would-be collectors is to what extent antiques and collectibles are investments. Generally speaking, if you decide to sell an object you can usually get your money back, plus an increment for inflation, especially if you are willing to wait a while before reselling. If you sell to a dealer, you will have to allow for his mark-up. If you decide to sell directly to private collectors you can ask a better price, but you will have to be willing to wait for a customer. Or you can, as many collectors do, have items auctioned off. Depending on how well you buy, you may do much better than get your money back, although of course it is possible to lose money, especially if you have bought into short-lived fads.

But it is not very interesting or rewarding for most people to buy antiques or collectibles as if they were pork bellies on the commodities exchange. For most people, buying antiques and collectibles does represent a very real investment, but in something that is rather more important: namely, in their homes. Such buying is an investment of time, thought and taste as well as money in order to enrich one's personal life.

You should be thinking of your purchases as long-term acquisitions. Do not wear yourself out hunting for bargains. Some of the worst purchases people make result from buying things which "look like bargains" but which on further study are not. Just as there can be no bargains in wilted vegetables, there are no bargains in inferior objects, no matter how inexpensive. Be willing to admit the gaps in your knowledge and be willing to do your homework before making major purchases. Then buy objects you can truly love and appreciate for what they are and what they represent. There is more satisfaction to be found in a few superb, enduring objects, than in many mediocre ones.

Insurance and Appraisals — Most commonly the question of an appraisal arises when you decide that your collection is valuable enough to insure. An appraisal may also be wise if you are selling a valuable collection, or are inheriting one.

How do you go about insuring a collection? Insurance companies have what is called a "personal articles floater". This floater allows coverage for particularly valuable personal property, such as jewelry, furs, camera equipment and "fine arts", which includes antiques and collectibles. In order to receive this coverage you will probably have to get a regular homeowners policy (which is also available for renters) as well. The advantage of insuring your antiques through a personal articles floater rather than through your regular homeowners insurance is that the premiums are much lower and there is no deductible. Also, unlike regularly insured items, it is assumed that items on the floater will maintain or increase in value. This assumption along with the documentation provided for each item should make it easier to collect in case of losses.

Each item on the floater is scheduled separately, described, and its value given. You must establish proof of ownership as well as the value of each item listed. A sales slip is adequate for both purposes, and if it accurately reflects the current value of the item being insured, then nothing more is needed. If, however, you made a particularly good buy, bought an item several years ago, or inherited a piece, then you will need an appraisal to establish its current worth.

How do you get an accurate appraisal? First, if you are a serious collector, you should have a fairly good idea of the value of the objects you have by keeping in touch with market prices. This is the best way you can ensure that an appraisal will be accurate. Secondly, you must find someone who is knowledgeable about the items that you collect. Your best bet is to consult a dealer who specializes in the categories you own. If you have a large collection in more than one area, it may be necessary to consult more than one person. If you do not know any such dealers, consult the decorative arts department of a museum near you for advice.

For an appraisal to be accurate, the appraiser must be able to identify the items and know their current values. No one person can be expected to know off-hand the value of a wide assortment of different things. Whoever is doing an appraisal will almost certainly have to do some research on at least some of the items being covered. Do not expect instant answers, and do expect to pay for professional services. Inquire about the charges beforehand, but expect to pay for each hour of labor required to complete the work.

Be particularly wary of appraisers who charge a percentage of the value of the items being appraised. This method is an open invitation to inflate the value of your collection. The purpose of an appraisal is to provide information, not flattery. If you overinsure your property the insurance company will be happy to pocket your premium, but it may be less tractable if you sustain a loss.

Notes to Part I

1. Sara Simonsgaard, "A Young Collector of American Glass", *National Antiques Review*, IV (June, 1973), p. 35.
2. Martha Gandy Fales, *Early American Silver* (New York: Dutton paper, 1973), p. ix.
3. *The Campbell Museum Collection* (Camden, New Jersey, 1969).
4. Elizabeth Stillinger, *The Antiques Guide to Decorative Arts in America: 1600–1875* (New York: E. P. Dutton & Co., Inc., 1972), p. 374.
5. From the Introduction by Alice Winchester, p. 9, in Jean Lipman and Alice Winchester, *The Flowering of American Folk Art: 1776–1876* (New York: The Viking Press, 1974).
6. Ibid.
7. Marshall B. Davidson, *The American Heritage History of Antiques from the Civil War to World War I* (New York: American Heritage Publishing Co., Inc., 1969), pp. 14–15.
8. As quoted by David A. Hanks in "The Arts and Crafts Movement in America, 1875-1916", *Antiques* CIV (August, 1973), p. 223.
9. Carl W. Drepperd, *ABC's of Old Glass* (New York: Award Books Paperback, 1968) p. 32.
10. Albert Sack, *Fine Points of Furniture: Early American* (New York: Crown Publishers, Inc., 1950).

PART II

Introductory Notes to Part II

This part of the book includes carefully selected lists of places where antiques and collectibles can be found. These lists, which are organized by states, include museums, shows, dealers, and auction houses, in that order. The reader will want to know how the various entries in each category came to be included.

The museums listed are ones that have especially good decorative arts collections. It has to be said that while many midwestern museums have substantial decorative arts collections, they have generally shown less interest in this area than the eastern museums. Better displays and more educational programs are badly needed. But whatever their shortcomings, you should by all means explore your local museums, and visit those listed in this book if you have the opportunity. Many museums, for the price of a membership fee, offer the collector very valuable privileges and services, including help in identifying antiques and use of the museum library.

My selection of individual dealers was influenced by three main factors. The first was personal knowledge. I have been an exhibitor at many good shows, which are excellent places to become acquainted with many dealers and their offerings. The best of these are included in the listings. Second, as a dealer I have come to know many shows and dealers by reputation; many of these have been included because they came highly recommended to me by reliable dealers and knowledgeable collectors who know them first hand. And third, I have taken into consideration membership in the National Association of Dealers in Antiques (NADA). This organization, the only national dealer's organization that is important in the Midwest, has done much to bring knowledge and integrity to the selling of antiques and collectibles in this area. The code of ethics to which members are asked to subscribe prohibits the knowing misrepresentation of goods, requires that everything for sale be clearly priced, and specifies that written descriptions of items sold must be furnished on request. Antique dealers are individualists, and many good ones, including many listed in this book, are not members of the NADA. (Nor are all Midwestern NADA members listed here.) Still, membership in this organization is one indication of professionalism and reliability.

Of course, it is inevitable, given this method of selection, that some excellent dealers and shows have been overlooked, and that many more dealers and shows that from time to time offer desirable merchandise, are not included. This is regretable, but my main purpose (rather than inclusiveness) has been to suggest places where even relatively inexperienced collectors can buy with confidence.

The reader will also wonder why some states seem, on the basis of these listings, to be much better represented in terms of dealers than others. A glance at the accompanying table of population growth will explain this seeming injustice. Those states with smaller populations, those settled later, and those with fewer large urban areas, are bound to be less well supplied with sources of antiques. This is not to say that every Midwestern state does not have a great deal to offer any collector.

The auction houses listed here, like the dealers, were selected on the basis of personal experience and what I have been able to learn of their reputations. They are listed last for each state because considerable knowledge is required

UNITED STATES BUREAU OF THE CENSUS

Admission of States to the Union		POPULATION OF STATES IN YEARS SHOWN						
		1800	1810	1820	1830	1840	1850	1970
Ohio	1803	45,365	230,760	581,434	937,903	1,519,467	1,980,329	10,652,017
Indiana	1816	5,641	24,520	147,178	343,031	685,866	988,416	5,193,669
Illinois	1818		12,282	55,211	157,445	476,183	851,470	11,113,976
Michigan	1837		4,762	8,896	31,639	212,267	397,654	8,875,083
Iowa	1846					43,112	192,241	2,824,376
Wisconsin	1848					30,945	305,391	4,417,731
Minnesota	1858						6,077	3,804,971

to buy from them successfully. However, this knowledge can be gained quite quickly, and they are definitely part of the fun of collecting. Here again it was not possible to list all of the good ones; if you wish to locate the best auctions and auctioneers in your area, ask the trust department at your bank for the names of the people they employ to conduct estate sales.

ILLINOIS

ILLINOIS MUSEUMS

THE ART INSTITUTE OF CHICAGO
Michigan Avenue and Adams St.
Chicago, IL 60603
Collections: European and American painting of all periods.
Sculpture, prints, drawings and photography. Decorative art
and textiles. Oriental art; Chinese, Japanese, Indian, and Middle
Eastern. An extensive art library.

CHICAGO HISTORICAL SOCIETY
Clark St. at North Ave.
Chicago, IL 60614
Collections: Costumes, weapons, American decorative arts;
American folk art, toys, dolls; American furniture, prints and
maps. Period rooms.

SPRINGFIELD ART ASSOCIATION
Edwards Place
700 N. 4th St.
Springfield, IL 62702
Collections: 19th and 20th cent. paintings; Oriental ceramics,
bronze, glass, and jewelry; early American furniture.
The Decorative Arts Museum is housed in Edwards Place,
the oldest house on its grounds in Springfield.

ILLINOIS SHOWS AND FLEA MARKETS

GREATER CHICAGO ANTIQUES SHOW
Saddle and Cycle Club
Foster Ave. and Lake Shore Drive
Chicago, IL
September
Information: Sponsored by the North Shore Jr. Board of the
Northwestern University Settlement.
Write: Northwestern University, Evanston, Illinois.

HINSDALE ANTIQUES SHOW
Hinsdale Community House
Madison and 8th Sts.
Hinsdale, IL 60521
Early September
Information: Write or call the Community House.

EMMANUEL EPISCOPAL CHURCH ANTIQUES SHOW
Emmanuel Episcopal Church
La Grange, IL 60525
Late February
Information: Call the office of the church.

LAKE FOREST STATION WAGON SHOW
Polo field on Westleigh Rd. (East of Hwy. 41)
Lake Forest, IL 60045
Early September
Information: This is a very high level flea market. Contact the
Lake Forest Center of the Infant Welfare Society of Chicago,
P.O. Box 23, Lake Forest, Illinois 60045.

LAKE FOREST ACADEMY—FERRY HALL ANTIQUES SHOW
1500 W. Kennedy Road
Lake Forest, IL 60045
Early June
Information: Call or write Lake Forest Academy — Ferry Hall.
Russell Carrell, Mgr. This is probably the most sumptuous
show in the Midwest.

HERITAGE SOCIETY ANTIQUES SHOW
Mercer Field House
North Central College
Naperville, IL 60540
Late October
Information: North Central College.

WAGON WHEEL ANTIQUES SHOW
Viking Auditorium
Rockton, IL
Early May and early November
Information: Contact George L. Miller, Show Director,
4805 Charles St., Rockton, IL 61108. This is an excellent show
with many out of state as well as Illinois dealers.

O'HARE NATIONAL ANTIQUES SHOW
O'Hare International Exposition and Trade Center
Rosemont, IL
August
Information: Contact Martin Ellis, Stratford Manor Shows,
5445 North California Ave., Chicago, IL 60625. (312) 588-1606.
A new show.

FOX VALLEY ANTIQUES SHOW
Kane County Fairgrounds
Randell Rd.
St. Charles, IL
March and October
Information: Contact Ralph G. Kennedy, Mgr., 409 N. Main St.,
Mt. Carroll, IL. (815) 244-9789. This show is produced by the
Chicago Suburban Antique Dealers Association, and any of
these dealers will be glad to give you information.

KANE COUNTY FLEA MARKET
Kane County Fairgrounds
Randell Rd.
St. Charles, IL
First Sunday of every month except for month of County Fair.
Information: Contact Mrs. J. L. Robinson, Mgr. (312) 232-2362.
Many good antiques and collectibles are to be found at this
flea market.

WILMETTE ANTIQUES SHOW
10th St. and Greenleaf Ave.
Wilmette, IL
Late October
Information: Contact Mrs. Charles T. Morrison, Mgr.,
2457 Prairie Ave., Evanston, IL 60091, or call the Woman's Club
of Wilmette, the sponsor. This is one of the oldest shows in the
area and a very good one.

THE WINNETKA COMMUNITY HOUSE ANTIQUES SHOW
620 Lincoln Ave.
Winnetka, IL 60093
Early March
Information: Contact the Winnetka Community House at the
address above.

ILLINOIS SHOPS

THE COURTYARD ANTIQUES
384½ Lake St.
P.O. Box X
Antioch, IL 60002
(312) 395-2766 or 395-0963
Jo Anna Larson
Hours: 10 to 4:30, closed Wed. and Sun.

General line, furniture, cut glass, treenware, country collectibles, Oriental rugs. NADA.

RUSNAK'S ANTIQUES
6338 W. 26th St.
Berwyn, IL 60402
(312) ST8-4086
John and Edward Rusnak
Hours: By chance or appointment.
Furniture, china, glass, metals, leaded glass lamps.

MARY BELL ANTIQUES
2405 S. Main St.
Bloomington, IL 61701
(309) 829-6497 or 662-4214
Marie Bishop
Hours: 1 to 5 daily.
General line, fine glass, china, furniture. Forty years in business, nine rooms and three garages full of antiques.
Appraisals and Estate Sales. NADA.

EARLY ATTIC
Corner of Cherry and Mill Sts.
Cedarville, IL 61013
(815) 563-4513
Ruth Simpert
Hours: 10 to 5 daily, closed Thursday.
Oak, pine, some in rough furniture; pottery. Rookwood to Roseville; pressed and cut glass; crocks, tools, woodenware, many old dishes. Main shop and large barn. NADA.

KENNETH NEBENZAHL, INC.
333 N. Michigan Ave.
Chicago, IL 60601
(312) 641-2711
Hours: 9 to 5 week days.
Rare books, maps, manuscripts and prints relating to the Western hemisphere.

CALLARD OF LONDON
100 E. Walton St.
Chicago, IL 60611
(312) 337-4320
P. W. Callard
Hours: 10 to 5.

Paintings, furniture, silver and decorative antique accessories.

JOSEPH E. DIMERY
739 N. Rush St.
Chicago, IL 60611
(312) SU7-3457
Mary Dimery Joerns and David W. Dimery
Hours: 10 to 5, appointment advisable.
A second generation dealer in English furniture and accessories with headquarters at Leeds, Yorkshire. Eighteenth and nineteenth century items, carefully selected.

MALCOLM FRANKLIN, INC.
126 E. Delaware Place
Chicago, IL 60611
(312) DE7-0202
Paul Mark Franklin and Mary Ann Sullivan Franklin
Hours: 9 to 5 Mon. through Sat. (closed Sat. in July and Aug.).
A second generation dealer (third generation now entering the business) internationally known for antique English furniture, porcelain, silver, and paintings.

DOROTHY G. HALE & CO.
904 N. Michigan Ave.
Chicago, IL 60611
(312) DE7-5955
Hours: 9 to 5 (closed Sat., July, Aug., Sept.).
English furniture, pewter, brass, glass; English and Continental porcelains.

WALTER H. WILSON, LTD.
904 N. Michigan Ave.
Chicago, IL 60611
(312) DE7-5955
Hours: 9 to 5 (closed Sat., July, Aug., Sept.).
Antique English silver and Old English silverplate.

JEAN F. LEWIS ANTIQUES
936 N. Michigan Ave., Room 306
Chicago, IL 60611
(312) 787-0985
Jean F. Lewis
Hours: 10 to 5, Mon. through Sat.
Eighteenth century English porcelain, Chinese export

porcelain, French faience, nineteenth century Rockingham,
stoneware, etc., unusual Oriental *objects d'art*.

TOM MENAUGH ANTIQUE FURNISHINGS
63 E. Oak St.
Chicago, IL 60611
(312) 664-9321
Tom Menaugh
Hours: 10 to 5, Tues. through Sat.
English and Continental furniture up to the early 19th century.

NAGATANI ORIENTAL ARTS
700 N. Michigan Ave.
Chicago, IL 60611
(312) 337-5449
Hours: Appointment necessary.
The finest in authenticated Oriental art objects.

TAYLOR B. WILLIAMS
P.O. Box 11297
Chicago, IL 60611
(312) 332-2475 (person to person).
Taylor B. Williams
Hours: By appointment only.
Authentic 18th and early 19th century American antique
furniture with complimenting accessories of the period;
for museums and the sophisticated collector.

GOLD COAST ANTIQUES, LTD.
154 E. Erie St., Suite 212
(312) 944-4424
Janet Raymond
Hours: 11 to 4:30 weekdays, 10 to 1 Sat. (but call first).
English 19th cent. and an assortment of French and American
furniture, lamps, fixtures, painting, samplers, etc.

WATER TOWER ANTIQUES, LTD.
154 E. Erie St., Suite 200
(312) 787-2752
Joan M. Schwartz
Hours: 11 to 4:30, Sat. by appointment.
Nineteenth century furniture, paintings, and fine cabinet pieces.

LA BOURSE
45 E. Walton Place
Chicago, IL 60611

(312) 787-3925
Hours: 10 to 5, Mon. through Sat.
An elegant antique shop run by the Woman's Board of the
Chicago Medical School.

MARSHALL FIELD & COMPANY
111 N. State St.
Chicago, IL 60690
This famous department store enjoys an international
reputation for quality and integrity. Perhaps less well known
is the fact that Fields offers in its downtown store an amazing
range of antiques. There are sixteen departments devoted to
antiques, and a very good selection of collectors' books in the
book department.

FIRST FLOOR

Antique Jewelry — The stock of 18th and 19th cent. jewelry in
this department, combined with the stock in the outlying
stores, amounts to the world's largest collection of antique
jewelry offered for sale. The countries of origin are America,
England, China, France, Holland, Russia, and Scotland.

The Antique Silver Shop — English silver from the early
Georgian through the Victorian and Edwardian periods;
antique Sheffield plate; American silver of the early and late
19th cent.

The Pewter Shop — 18th and early 19th cent. American and
English pewter; some Britannia and Continental pewter.
Modern pewter is also sold here, and can be helpfully compared
to the old.

Antique Clocks — Many types of decorative clocks in metal,
including carriage clocks.

Fields Afar — A changing selection of antique decorative
accessories from around the world.

SECOND FLOOR

Antiques and Artwares Gallery — 18th and 19th cent. English
soft- and hard-paste porcelain, early English creamware and
stone china, English and Continental glass, "Vieux Paris"
porcelain.

Oriental Gallery — Antiques from Southeast Asia; porcelains,
jades, old Japanese Imari, bronzes and carvings; Chinese

coromandel screens; painted and inlaid screens from Japan and Hong Kong.

Decorative Ceramics — Limited editions.

THIRD FLOOR

In various departments on this floor you will find rare books, prints, maps, autographs, and fine bindings; coins; stamps; collectors books.

FOURTH FLOOR

Toys — Antique dolls, trains, model soldiers, banks, minatures.

EIGHTH FLOOR

The Antiques Gallery — 17th, 18th, and early 19th cent. English and Continental furniture; English and Continental hard-paste porcelain; English soft-paste porcelain; English and Continental earthenwares of the 18th and early 19th cent.; period decorative accessories.

The Crossroads Market — Furniture and accessories from the Georgian and Victorian periods in wood, pottery, glass, brass, etc.

American Antiques — 17th, 18th, and early 19th cent. formal and country furniture, paintings, prints, primitives, pottery, copper, brass, tole, and other decorative accessories of these periods.

ANTIQUE PRINTS
1816 N. Wells St.
Chicago, IL 60614
(312) 642-1703
David H. Gee
Hours: By appointment only, weekday evenings.
A wide variety of prints from early 17th cent. to later Victorian; some orientals (woodcuts) ; some American steel engravings.

COLLECTORS NOOK
1714 N. Wells St.
Chicago, IL 60614
(312) 642-4734

Edith E. Lipsky
Hours: 1 to 5, Mon. through Sat., or by appointment.
American and European furniture, country English furniture;
primitives, accessories and collectors items.

FLY-BY-NITE GALLERY
714 N. Wells St.
Chicago, IL 60610
(312) 664-8136
Thomas M. Tomc
Hours: By appointment, 10 to 5, except Sun.
Pre-Raphaelite, Symbolist, Decadent, *Jugend Stil*, Arts and
Crafts, Art Nouveau, Secessionist, Aesthetic Movement,
Exoticism, Art Deco, *Die Wiener Werkstatte, Art Moderne,*
Advertising Arts.

MARK & LOIS JACOBS AMERICAN COLLECTIBLES
702 N. Wells St.
Chicago, IL 60610
(312) 787-8027
Mark and Lois Jacobs
Hours: 10 to 5 Mon. through Fri., 10 to 4 Sat.
Political items, antique advertising, breweriana, sports
memorabilia, radio premiums, comic and character items,
postcards, valentines, comic books, World's Fair souvenirs,
paper Americana.

JOSEPH W. FELL, LTD.
3221 N. Clark St.
Chicago, IL 60657
(312) 549-6076
Joseph W. Fell
Hours: 10 to 5 Tues. through Sat. (or by appointment).
A specialist in antique rugs and textiles. Collector's rugs,
kilims, Caucasian rugs. Room and scatter sizes.

MARDON ANTIQUES
3227 N. Clark St.
Chicago, IL 60657
(312) 281-1807
Donald Rose
Hours: 12 to 6, appointment recommended.
Choice cut glass, turn of the century porcelains and other
decorative objects of the period. NADA.

PATRICIA H. WILLEMS
Chicago, IL
(312) 973-2043
Patricia H. Willems
Hours: By appointment only.
Fine art objects.

CHARLES FRAHM LTD.
Chicago, IL 60615
(312) 373-2358 or 642-7464
Nancy Frahm
Hours: By appointment only.
Irish Georgian, Regency, and Victorian furniture, Oriental
rugs; old quilts; English and American antiques; copper.

S. WOLBERG ANTIQUES
1006 S. Michigan Ave.
Chicago, IL 60605
(312) 922-1939, after 6 call 973-4771.
S. Wolberg
Hours: 10 to 4 week days by appointment.
Fine late 19th and 20th cent. porcelains: Meissen, Dresden,
Minton, Coalport, and others; art and colored glass of the late
19th and early 20th cent.; jewelry, Mettlach steins and plaques.

YANKEE PEDDLER ANTIQUES
Village Square, 211 W. Burlington
Clarendon Hills, IL 60514
(312) 654-9043
Susan Tanner and Myrna Mohler
Hours: 10 to 4 Tues. through Sat.
Country furniture, decorative accessories, advertising items,
toys, tins.

HAND-E-CRAFT SHOP ANTIQUES
417 Arnold Rd.
East Peoria, IL 61611
(309) 699-2048
Wayne and Louise Abercrombie
Hours: 9 to 4:30.
Early china and glass, coverlets, quilts, metals; early country
furniture with accessories of the period. NADA.

GALERIE DE PORCELAINE
P.O. Box 293

Elmhurst, IL 60126
Marion Zickefoose
Hours: Mail order only.
Haviland matching and sets. Send sample or Schleiger number.

HOUSE OF ANTIQUES
314 E. State St.
Geneva, IL 60134
(312) 232-9650
Jeanne and Marvin Smith
Hours: 10 to 5, closed Mon.
Eighteenth and early nineteenth cent. American furniture and
accessories; flow blue and flow mulberry china; tealeaf and
white ironstone. NADA.

THE 1848 HOUSE
121 W. State St.
Geneva, IL 60134
(312) 232-9546
Bill D. Kohanek and W. Harvey Hoeppner
Hours: 11 to 5 Tues. through Sat., Sun. by chance.
Excellent early furniture and accessories.

SHIRLEY McGILL ANTIQUES
717 E. State St.
Geneva, IL 60134
(312) 232-4196
Hours: 10 to 4 Tues. through Sat., 12 to 4 Sun.
American pre-Civil War country furniture in pine, cherry,
walnut, etc.; pewter, iron, brass, copper; quilts, pressed glass,
Currier and Ives lithographs.

LAWRENCE L. ZIMMERMAN ANTIQUES
942 E. State St.
Geneva, IL 60134
(312) 232-8252
Hours: By appointment.
Excellent early antiques.

THE SWAN HOUSE
122 N. Sycamore St.
Genoa, IL 60135
(815) 784-5537
Janice G. Campbell
Hours: 1 to 6 Fri. through Sun. (except during shows);

otherwise by chance or appointment.
Nineteenth cent. country furniture in pine, cherry, walnut, and original paint; also accessories with emphasis on tin. NADA.

THE ANTIQUE GALLERY
482 Duane St.
Glen Ellyn, IL 60137
(312) 469-3555
Helen W. Gray
Hours: 1 to 4 Tues. through Fri., 10 to 4 Sat.
Paintings, prints, Orientalia, collectibles, furniture "in the rough", jewelry, textiles. NADA.

CAP COD HOUSE
439 Pennsylvania Ave.
Glen Ellyn, IL 60137
(312) 858 0040
Margaret Landies
Hours: 10 to 4 Tues. through Sat., 12 to 5 Sun.
Furniture, primitives, lamps, and pattern glass.

NADINE P. MARTENS
522 Hillside Ave.
Glen Ellyn, IL 60137
(312) 858-9249
Hours: 10 to 4 Tues. through Sat. or by appointment.
Select 18th and 19th cent. furnishings and interiors, including fabrics, floor coverings, papers, lighting (country and formal); American and English.

BETTY PITTS ANTIQUES
22 W. 640 Burr Oak Drive
Glen Ellyn, IL 60137
(312) 469-3643
Hours: By appointment or chance.
Dolls, jewelry, furniture, primitives, Estate Sales conducted.

THE VILLAGE ANTIQUARIAN
475 Hawthorne St.
Glen Ellyn, IL 60137
(312) 858-1568
Judy Marks
Hours: By appointment only.
Early American primitives and country furniture.

ALADDIN'S LAMP ANTIQUES
1913 Sheridan Rd.
Highland Park, IL 60035
(312) 432-0439
Herman and Rosemary Wren
Hours: 10 to 5.
Seventeen rooms of antique and collectible items, from
American estates and imports from all over the world. Clock
room has over 200 clocks. 100,000 items from $1 to $7500. NADA.

BARBARA CURTIS ANTIQUES
5900 Grant St.
Hinsdale, IL 60521
(312) 323-7914
Barbara Curtis
Hours: 11 to 4 Tues. through Sat., by appointment Sun.
Country furniture, English and American decorative
accessories.

PLATINUM ALLEY
17938 S. Halsted St.
Homewood, IL 60430
(312) 798-9776
Jim and Barbara
Hours: 12 to 6 every day except Mon.
Antique jewelry, clocks and watches (also repairs);
general line of antiques and collectibles.

THE ANTIQUE EMPORIUM
640 Greenbay Rd.
Kenilworth, IL 60043
(312) 251-6090
Susan D. Grahm and Vincent J. Grahm, Jr.
Hours: 10:30 to 4:30 Tues. through Sat.
English furniture and accessories; paintings restored.

THE FEDERALIST ANTIQUES
523 Park Drive
Kenilworth, IL 60043
(312) 256-1791
Michael S. Corbett
Hours: 10 to 4:30 Tues. through Sat. or by appointment.
American furniture 1770 to 1830; American silver, paintings,

brass; fine period lighting; English ceramics and Chinese porcelain.

SNOW-GATE ANTIQUES, INC.
654 N. Bank Lane
Lake Forest, IL 60045
Mrs. Cris Lagoria
Hours: 10 to 4:45 Mon. through Sat.
Antique jewelry, general line of collectibles including glass, china, brass, etc.

SPRUCE ANTIQUES, LTD.
188 E. Westminster
Lake Forest, IL 60045
(312) 234-0221
Jone R. Gedge and Virginia M. Briggs
Hours: By appointment.
Eighteenth and nineteenth cent. English furniture and decorative accessories.

ARNOLD MARCUS CHERNOFF, LTD.
29 Londonderry Lane
Lincolnshire (Deerfield), IL 60015
(312) 945-7200
Arnold Marcus Chernoff
Hours: By appointment only.
Large range of firearms for collectors and museums; American Indian beadwork, weapons, and other artifacts.

THE WALRUS QUILT SHOP
175 Half Day Rd.
Lincolnshire (Prairie Road P.O.), IL 60069
(312) 634-0170
Barbara Benson and Barbara Leech
Hours: By appointment Mon. through Sat.
Quilts for sale and to order quilting; quilting lessons, supplies, and services; quilted accessories.

STONEHOUSE ANTIQUES
614 W. Murry St.
Macomb, IL 61455
(309) 833-5362
Verda Shake
Hours: 9 to 5.
Walnut and pine furniture; primitives and lamps.

WINDSOR HOUSE ANTIQUES
1 Heath Court, Stratford West
Macomb, IL 61455
(309) 836-2861
Paul W. Blackford
Hours: By appointment.
Country painted and country formal furniture; historical
Staffordshire and other early china; American folk art.

BURTON'S ANTIQUES
402 N. 4th St.
Marshall, IL 62441
(217) 826-8736
Keith and Marty Burton
Hours: By appointment or chance.
Furniture and primitives; stoneware, some glass and china;
country furniture.

PUFFABELLY STATION
Hwy. 136, (1 Block N. of Rt. 66).
McLean, IL 61754
(309) 874-3161
Rebecca Beeler and Carol Lystad
Hours: 10 to 5 Fri. through Mon. (Closed Jan.).
General line; primitives, furniture, glassware, china,
railroad items, turquoise. NADA.

LAWRENCE E. (Gene) KING
Main St., Box 38
Monroe Center, IL 61052
(815) 393-4735
Gene King
Hours: By chance or appointment.
Furniture, ceramics, glass, metals, from late 17th cent. to
late Victorian; fine Americana. NADA.

BONNIE'S BYGONES
530 White Oak Dr.
Naperville, IL 60540
(312) 355-2863
Bonnie Cosyns
Hours: By appointment.
Nineteenth cent. furniture of all periods; small primitives and
early Americana in stoneware, ironstone; lighting and related
items.

KERIN DEE ANTIQUES
522 Belleforte Ave.
Oak Park, IL 60302
(312) EU6-6227
Kerin Dee
Hours: By mail order or appointment.
Lamps, pattern glass.

BETTY GRISSOM ANTIQUES
602 W. Maywood
Peoria, IL 61604
(309) 685-0841
John and Betty Grissom
Hours: By appointment.
Fine art glass, 18th and 19th cent. porcelain and pottery,
primitives; insurance appraisals for fine arts and antiques.
NADA.

MY HOUSE ANTIQUES
1003 E. Camp McDonald Rd.
Prospect Heights, IL 60070
(312) 392-0383
June Johnson
Hours: 12 to 6, closed Mon.
Fine art glass, cut glass, porcelains, jewelry; some Mid-
Victorian furniture; lamps and paintings. Everything sold on
money back guarantee regarding authenticity. Appraisals.
NADA.

THE COLLECTORS
9 N. Parkway
Prospect Heights, IL 60070
(312) 255-0484
Joanne Kuhns
Hours: By appointment.
Midwestern country furniture in pine, poplar, butternut;
baskets and early farm tools, textile items.

THE HALLWAY ANTIQUES
145 Vine Ave.
Park Ridge, IL 60068
(312) 696-2891
Dorothy Hinkley
Hours: 10 to 4 Tues. and Thurs., 11 to 2 Sat.
Country furniture, primitives, stoneware, baskets, quilts,
and related small antiques.

SENTIMENTAL JOURNEY ANTIQUES
P.O. Box 82
Park Ridge, IL 60068
(312) 698-2669
Sharon and Dean De Ogny
Hours: By appointment only.
A specialist in superior American Brilliant Period cut glass.

THE EAGLES NEST
7080 Old River Rd. (RR6)
Rockford, IL 61103
(815) 633-8410
C. Richard Franke
Hours: 10 to 6 daily.
Country furniture, primitives, glass, china, and
general line. Several buildings and show-rooms. NADA.

THE LOFT COUNTRY STORES
5859 N. Main Rd.
Rockford, IL 61103
(815) 877-1958
Shirley and Charles Kowing
Hours: 10 to 5 daily, 12 to 5 Sun.
Small furniture, glass, china, copper and brass, jewelry,
prints. NADA.

THE RED ONION
4805 Charles St.
Rockford, IL 61108
(815) 399-7624
Evelyn and George Miller
Hours: 10 to 5 or by appointment.
Rope beds, tiger maple, pine, etc.; walnut cupboards,
secretaries, small tables, etc.; books; many whale oil lamps.
The Millers are the show managers of the Wagon Wheel
Antique Show. NADA.

RED ROOSTER
Wagon Wheel
Rockton, IL 61072
(815) 624-7011
D. J. Pleuss and E. J. Vaughn
Hours: By appointment or chance.
Antique jewelry.

HILLCROFT
1147 Geneva Rd.
St. Charles, IL 60174
(312) 584-4001
Robert T. Zohbel
Hours: By appointment only.
Fine early antiques.

FRANCES FORREST ANTIQUES
Rt. 1
Sandoval, IL 62882
(618) 775-8444
Frances Forrest
Hours: By appointment or chance.
Furniture, china, glass, primitives.

AARDVARK CLOCKS AND ANTIQUES
1406 S. 5th St.
Springfield, IL 62703
(217) 789-1129
Estella P. Booth
Hours: 10 to 5 daily, 12 to 5 Sun.
Clocks, furniture, glassware, primitives, general line. **NADA.**

BONNIE'S CARRIAGE HOUSE ANTIQUES
U.S. 54
Summer Hill, IL 62370
(217) 285-4557
Bonnie Wombles
Hours: By appointment.
Early American and country furniture; woodenware, iron and
tin ware; coverlets, china, pattern glass, stoneware; good
early primitives; oak and Victorian furniture.

VIOLETTA'S
128 W. St., Charles Rd.
Villa Park, IL 60181
(312) 834-4444
Violetta R. Johnson
Hours: 10:30 to 4:30 Tues., Wed., Thurs., Sat.; 1 to 5 Sun.
Pattern glass, furniture, silver, jewelry, art glass,
primitives, dolls. Two floors, unusually well filled.

WILLOW BROOK FARM
Village of Milburn on Rt. 45

Wadsworth, IL 60083
(312) 356-3022 or 356-3728
Rita Murphy and Patricia Lamkin
Hours: 10 to 4 daily except Mon.
Antiques and decorator items.

MARY RACHEL ANTIQUE SHOP
501 Walnut
Washington, IL 61571
(309) 283-2911
Harold and Mary Levery
Hours: 10 to 5 Mon. through Sat.; 1 to 5 Sun.
Large shop with a general line of antiques; china, pressed
glass, silver, jewelry, art glass, figurines, clocks, lamps, trays,
primitives, bottles, Victorian and country furniture. NADA.

THE LITTLE CORNER, INC.
117 Bangs
Wauconda, IL 60084
(312) 526-8452
Lee and Jim Hoekje
Hours: 10 to 5 daily, 12 to 5 Sun.
Dolls, jewelry, 19th and 20th cent. original posters, china,
glass, silver. Doll hospital; clock repair; antique appraisals.
NADA.

THE ROBIN'S NEST
416 Slocum Rd.
Wauconda, IL 60084
(312) 526-5255
Dee Wenborg
Hours: 12 to 4 daily except Mon. and Tues.
A specialist in Victorian furniture (American origin) restored,
quality pieces only; some American country pine furniture.
NADA.

CANDLELIGHT ANTIQUES
126 Chestnut (Rt. 17)
Wenona, IL 61764
(815) 844-5645
Chuck and Louise Young
Hours: 9:30 to 5 Mon., Wed., Fri.
Art, cut and pressed glass (especially pressed pattern glass);
furniture, china, primitives, jewelry, dolls. NADA.

BULL AND BEAR ANTIQUES
406 Linden Ave.
Wilmette, IL 60091
(312) 256-6626
Frank H. Gazzolo
Hours: 10 to 5 Tues. through Sat.
Russian icons and works of art; English furniture; fine
English and European clocks; Russian and English books on
the fine arts. Catalogue available.

PHILLIP TRIER
714 Central St.
Wilmcttc, IL 60091
(312) 256-4147
Phillip Trier
Hours: By appointment.
Country furniture, early American blown glass, pottery, folk
art, paintings, hooked rugs, quilts. A specialist in Illinois
antiques.

HOPE CARROLL
202 N. Water St.
Wilmington, IL 60481
(815) 476-2746
Hope Rajala and Carol Lewis
Hours: 1 to 5 Tues. through Fri.; 11 to 5 Sat.
Primitives, country furniture, interesting wood objects,
pattern glass.

CALEDONIAN, INC.
562 Lincoln Ave.
Winnetka, IL 60093
(312) 446-6566 and 446-0912
Hours: 9 to 5 Tues. through Sat.
Eighteenth and early ninctcenth cent. English furniture and
accessories; mahogany and oak furniture; china, pewter,
brass, copper, oil paintings, prints, clocks, barometers.

DOMINIQUE COUNTRY FRENCH ANTIQUES
899 Linden Ave.
Winnetka, IL 60093
(312) 446-0584
Dominique Del Medico
Hours: 10 to 5 Mon. through Sat.

Country French furniture imported from French provinces.

GEORGETTE ANTIQUES
897½ Linden Ave.
Winnetka, IL 60093
(312) 446-5515
Georgette Burnett
Hours: 11 to 4:30 Tues. through Fri.; Sat. by appointment.
English and American country furniture; porcelain and other
decorative accessories; fine needlework.

THE LION MARK
721 Elm St. — P.O. Box 276
Winnetka, IL 60093
(312) 446-8448
Charles W. Packer and Virginia W. Packer
Hours: 10 to 5 Tues. through Sat., but call ahead.
Antique English silver of the highest quality.

ILLINOIS AUCTIONS

HANZEL GALLERIES, INC.
William Hanzel
1120 S. Michigan Ave.
Chicago, IL 60605
(312) 922-6234

DIRECT AUCTIONEERS
7232 N. Western Ave.
Chicago, IL 60645
(312) 465-3300

DUNNINGS AUCTION SERVICE
822 Oakley, P.O. Box 866
Elgin, IL 60120
(312) 741-3483
Terry Dunning
Mailing address: 30 W. Washington St., #1432, Chicago, IL
60602

DOUGLAS BOOMGARDEN
Davis Junction, IL 61020
(815) 393-4417

ED ATKINSON AUCTIONEER
Manhattan, IL 60442
(815) 469-4642

HENDERSON AUCTION SERVICE
Mazon, IL 60444
(815) 448-2488

DWAINE AND DON BAUER
Windsor, IL 61957
(217) 459-2696

INDIANA

INDIANA MUSEUMS

INDIANAPOLIS MUSEUM OF ART
1200 W. 38th St.
Indianapolis, IN 46208
Collections: Painting, sculptures, textiles, ceramics, and silver.
The Lilly Pavilion of Decorative Arts.

SHELDON SWOPE ART GALLERY
25 S. 7th St.
Terre Haute, IN 47807
Collections: 19th and 20th cent. painting and sculpture;
drawings, prints, and decorative arts; modern European glass.
1700 volume art and reference library.

INDIANA SHOWS

CRUTCHER INDIANAPOLIS REAL ANTIQUE SHOW
Indiana State Fairgrounds
1900 E. 38th St. (US36)
Indianapolis, IN

April and Oct.; June and December
Information: If you wish to be put on the mailing list, write
Jean Crutcher, Mgr., Rt. 1, 7370 Old National Trail E., New
Carlisle, Ohio 45344. Jean Crutcher's shows are nationally
famous, primarily because of their very high quality and
professionalism, but also because they have several characteristics which make them especially attractive to collectors and
dealers. First, everything is guaranteed; any object purchased,
if it is in the same condition as when purchased, can be returned
(within six months) to the dealer and the full price refunded,
without question. Second, since the shows are not sponsored by
a charitable organization, previews, program booklets and
other expensive distractions can be dispensed with, and effective
advertising supplied in their place. For this reason the shows
are very heavily attended both by dealers and collectors.

There are two separate biannual Crutcher Indianapolis
shows, although they both have the same name and address.
The April and October show was the first established, and it
has become such a fixture that the U.S. Dept. of Commerce
lists it in a directory that is distributed around the world. The
June and December show was added to accommodate the many
dealers for whom space could not be found in the original show.
No dealers are allowed to exhibit in both.

These are huge shows in a very large facility: over 130
dealers, as many as 40,000 people in attendance over four days.

ALLIANCE ANTIQUE SHOW
510 N. New Jersey St.
Indianapolis, IN
June
Information: Write Mrs. L. J. Bruner, 7731 Conifer Court,
Indianapolis, IN 46250. Sponsored by the Alliance of the
Indianapolis Museum of Art, John Fifield, Mgr.

ORIGINAL FORT WAYNE ANTIQUE SHOW
Exhibition Hall, Memorial Coliseum
Parnell Ave. (US 30 By-Pass)
Fort Wayne, IN
Spring and Fall.
Information: Write Frank R. Palmer, Mgr., Mt. Vernon, Ohio
43050. Sponsored by Psi Iota Xi of Fort Wayne.

INDIANA SHOPS

FLO'S ANTIQUES, THE HOUSE OF NIPPON
5904 Pendleton Ave.
Anderson, IN 46011
(317) 643-4541
Ray and Flo Meyer
Hours: 9 to 5 Sat. and Sun., and by appointment.
Specializing in Nippon, hat pins and stickpins; general line of
good quality porcelain, Victorian silver, clocks. Flo Meyer
is the author of *The House of Nippon* and *Pins for Hats and
Cravats*. NADA.

WM. G. NEPTUNE ANTIQUES
Box 54
Brooklyn, IN 46111
William and Lela E. Neptune
Hours: Please write for appointment.
Blown art glass such as Steuben (before 1932), Tiffany, Quezal,
Durand, T. Webb, S.&W., plus European glass; pattern glass
1840–1900; small lamps, chandelier sets; iridized and
decorated glass shades; costume jewelry the owners have made
from pieces of Tiffany, Steuben, etc.; some blown molded
early glass.

ACORN FARM ANTIQUES
15466 Oak Rd.
Carmel, IN 46032
(317) 846-2383
Herb, Dee, and Judee Sweet
Hours: 10 to 5 Tues. through Sat.
Furniture, oil paintings, silver and good primitives. **NADA.**

STEPHEN AND BETTY JONES
RR2, Box 61
Centerville, IN 47330
(317) 855-3610
Hours: By appointment.
Fine 18th and 19th cent. furniture and accessories.

CURREY'S ANTIQUES
RR9, Squawbuck Rd. (Corner of Lincoln Hwy. and Squawbuck)
Columbia City, IN 46725
(219) 244-3636

Carol Currey
Hours: Daily and evenings by chance or appointment.
Country furniture, decorated and painted furniture, primitives,
men's collectibles, decoys, samplers, early baskets, postcards.

LOUISE'S ANTIQUES
8360 W. Delphi Pike 27
Converse, IN 46919
(317) 395-3579
Louise Boyd
Hours: 8 to 6, a call ahead advised.
Greentown, art glass, general line. The owner is a show
manager and the author of *Greentown in Color*. NADA.

P. MICHELS JONES STUDIO
402 S. John St.
Crawfordsville, IN 47933
(317) 362-8236
Paul Jones, Jr.
Hours: By chance or appointment seven days a week.
French, English, and formal American furniture; some
Victorian furniture, chandeliers, other lighting fixtures;
decorative accessories; shutters, doors, and other
architectural fragments; paintings.

LEONA G. CROUCH ANTIQUES AND INTERIORS
404 E. Main St. (Hwy. 25)
Delphi, IN 46923
(317) 564-4195
Leona G. Crouch
Hours: 11 to 6, closed Thurs. morning; appointment advised.
Fine porcelains and art glass, Victorian jewelry, fine period
furniture. Everything is guaranteed. NADA.

ANNETTE'S ANTIQUES
6910 Lincoln Highway East
Fort Wayne, IN 46803
(219) 749-2745
Annette R. Latker
Hours: 1 to 5 Sat. and Sun., otherwise by chance or appointment.
Fine porcelain and glass (art, colored, and pressed) a specialty;
dolls, lamps, primitives, and decorative pieces; furniture, early
pattern glass, bottles. NADA.

RUTH'S ANTIQUES
502 W. Main St.
Greentown, IN 46936
(317) 628-3895
Ruth P. Campbell
Hours: 10 to 6, evenings by appointment.
Orientals a specialty; general line; Greentown Glass, small
pieces of furniture and primitives. **NADA.**

COUNTRY ANTIQUES SHOPPE
RR 1, Box 109
Huntington, IN 46750
(219) 344-2858
Garr and Elsie Kitt
Hours: By appointment.
Art glass, colored glass, china, dolls, lamps, jewelry, postcards.
NADA.

GOLDEN RULE ANTIQUE SHOP
9600 E. Washington (US 40)
Indianapolis, IN 46229
(317) 897-4080
Ronald Cox
Hours: 10 to 6, 12 to 6 Sun.
Specializing in Victorian furniture; also china, glass. Large
selection of new books on antiques. Stripping service. **NADA.**

HIGGINBOTHAM ANTIQUES
Box 55104
Indianapolis, IN 46205
(317) 255-2300
Ed Higginbotham
Hours: By appointment; shows.
Coins, antique guns, Civil War items.

OPAL SALEE ANTIQUES
1600 South Armstrong
Kokomo, IN 46901
(317) 457-2482
Opal Salee
Hours: By appointment.
Art glass, cut glass, china. NADA.

JIM AND TAMSIE McCORMICK
40 S. Ohio St.

Martinsville, IN 46151
(317) 342-6177
Jim and Tamsie McCormick
Hours: By appointment.
Painted country furniture and accessories, especially of the
period 1800–50.

LUCY AND I ANTIQUES
802 S. Main St.
Monticello, IN 47960
(219) 583-7652
Dicie M. Lucy
Hours: By appointment or chance.
Fine mechanical banks; Victorian furniture to 1910; rare
colored and clear pattern glass; lamps, clocks, primitives in
kitchen and farm tools.

WHAT NOT HOUSE
2515 W. Adams St.
Muncie, IN 47302
Virginia Thornburg
Hours: Write for an appointment.
Quality 18th and 19th cent. antiques only; glass, china,
furniture, metals, fabrics, paper. Everything guaranteed.

THE ESCHENBACHS ANTIQUES
8835 Northcote Ave.
Munster, IN 46321
(219) 838-5227
Robert and Virginia Eschenbachs
Hours: By appointment; shows.
Primitives, wood, iron, copper, tin, brass, all completely
renovated.

JAY AND ELLEN CARTER ANTIQUES
P.O. Box 252
Nashville, IN 47448
(812) 988-7904
Jay and Ellen Carter
Hours: By appointment or chance.
Eighteenth and nineteenth cent. furniture, the majority in the
old paint; Shaker furniture and accessories; stoneware,
redware, quilts, coverlets, early lighting devices, treenware;
Indian baskets and rugs.

FRANKLIN SCHUELL
51027 Portage Rd.
South Bend, IN 46628
(219) 272-9310
Hours: By appointment only.
Paperweights, antique and modern; fine antique miniatures,
portraits painted on ivory.

LOST CAUSE ANTIQUES GALLERY
Main at Main Cross
Vevay, IN 47043
(812) 427-2900
Ann Farnfley
Hours: 12 to 5 Fri., Sat., Sun., or by appointment.
American primitive furniture, paintings, and old prints;
art pottery, copper, and brass.

INDIANA AUCTIONS

MUDD GALLERIES
1250 Washington St.
Columbus, IN 47201
(812) 372-2553

ELLENBERGER BROTHERS
7410 Bluffton Rd.
Fort Wayne, IN 46714
(219) 747-3189

LEWIS AND LAMBRIGHT
112 N. Detroit St.
La Grange, IN 46761
(219) 463-2013

IOWA

IOWA MUSEUMS

ROBERT LUCAS PLUM GROVE HOUSE
727 Switzer Ave.
Iowa City, Iowa 52240
Collections: Period furnishings. Robert Lucas was the first
governor of the Territory of Iowa.

DEPARTMENT OF HISTORY AND ARCHIVES
E. 12th and Grand Ave.
Des Moines, Iowa 50319
Collections: China, glass, silver, guns, toys and dolls; extensive
history and geneological library.

SALISBURY HOUSE
4025 Tonawanda Dr.
Des Moines, Iowa 50312
Collections: 15th through 17th cent. furnishings, tapestries, and
paintings are displayed in this historic house built in 1923–28.

IOWA SHOWS

CAPITAL CITY ANTIQUE SHOW
Holiday Inn
6111 Fleur Dr.
Des Moines, Iowa
Spring and Fall.
Information: Contact Helen Fortier, Mgr., Allenspark,
Colorado 80510.
(303) 586-4762.

CEDAR RAPIDS ANTIQUE SHOW
Veterans Memorial Coliseum
Cedar Rapids, Iowa
Spring and Fall.
Information: Donald C. Koehn, Mgr., 5100 Johnson Ave., Cedar
Rapids, Iowa 52404.

OTTUMWA IOWA ANTIQUE SHOW
YWCA Bldg.
Ottumwa, Iowa
March
Information: Don Williams, Mgr., 2753 N. Court, Ottumwa,
Iowa 52501.

IOWA SHOPS

AGNES KOEHN ANTIQUES
5100 Johnson Ave., S. W.
Cedar Rapids, Iowa 52404
(319) 396-3836
Donald C. Koehn
Hours: 10 to 4 daily.
Art glass and fine colored glass; **French cameo glass and French
dolls a specialty. NADA.**

BURKART ANTIQUES
908 Rhomberg Ave., P.O. Box 282
Dubuque, Iowa 52001
(319) 582-2537
Helen Burkart
Hours: By chance or appointment.
A general line of antiques. NADA.

THE LANTERN ANTIQUES
300 Main St.
La Porte City, Iowa 50651
(319) 342-2024
Ron and Laura Fultz
Hours: 10 to 5 Tues. through Sat.
Furniture, primitives, glass, china.

CHESTER N. SHEETS ANTIQUES
106 N. Dearborn
Maquoketa, Iowa 52060
(319) 652-2334
Chester Sheets
Hours: By appointment.
Pressed glass and china a specialty. **Everything guaranteed.**

RED ROBIN FARM
Rt. 3 (Hwy. 212)
Marengo, Iowa 52301
(319) 642-5450
Mrs. Kenneth McCune
Hours: By chance or appointment.
New England country pine furniture and accessories; painted
furniture; some period lighting and hand woven rugs;
no oak or collectibles.

ORIGINAL ANTIQUE SHOP
933 8th Ave.
Marion, Iowa 52302
(319) 377-1130
Mrs. J. J. Monn
Hours: 10 to 5 daily except Sun.
Early French Haviland (sets and pieces), cut glass, hand
painted china, pattern glass, milk glass, art glass;
small collectibles.

THE WOODEN HORSE
117 Main St.
Mount Vernon, Iowa 52314
(319) 895-8980
Daisy C. Beckhelm (Mrs. Paul)
Hours: 10 to 5:30 daily, Sun. by appointment.
Early Victorian furniture, "Penn. type" primitives, silver,
early pressed glass, tin, china, early advertising items,
paperweights, music manuscripts.

R & K WEENIKE ANTIQUES
Rt. 7
Ottumwa, Iowa 52501
(515) 934-5427
Roy and Kathleen Weenike
Hours: By chance or appointment.
General line including pattern, cut, and some art glass; some
furniture, hand painted china. Mr. Weenike grinds and repairs
antique glass.

THE VICTORIAN HOUSE
211 6th St.
Parkersburg, Iowa 50665
(319) 346-2511

Rose Brooks and Ethel Meikle
Hours: By appointment.
Art glass, pattern glass, dolls, jewelry, furniture. NADA.

HEAVENLY DAZE ANTIQUES
122 E. First St.
Sumner, Iowa 50674
(515) 224-3227
Helen M. Miller
Hours: 10 to 5 weekdays, 1 to 5 Sun.
General line, refinished furniture, china, glass, lamps, clocks, brass, copper, primitives. NADA.

HOFREITER'S ANTIQUES INC.
4025 University Ave.
Waterloo, Iowa 50701
(319) 233-3691
R. G. Hofreiter
Hours: 10 to 5 weekdays, 10 to 4 Sat.
Art glass, lamps, china, furniture (mainly finished); Victorian furniture reproductions. Lamps repaired, silk and glass shades made. NADA.

THE SHOP IN THE VILLAGE ANTIQUES
West Branch, Iowa 52358
(319) 643-2513
Dale and Mary Van Ginkle
Hours: 9:30 to 5 daily, 11 to 5 Sun.
Fine American antiques.

IOWA AUCTIONS

GENE HARRIS
Box 294
203 S. 18th Ave.
Marshalltown, Iowa 50158
(515) 752-0600

WAYNE STEWART AUCTIONEER
812 Brookside Dr.
Audubon, Iowa 50025
(712) 563-3549

MICHIGAN

MICHIGAN MUSEUMS

DETROIT INSTITUTE OF ART
5200 Woodward Ave.
Detroit, MI 48202
Collections: European paintings, sculptures, graphic art, decorative art and textiles. Period rooms, costumes, Indian artifacts.

GREENFIELD VILLAGE AND THE HENRY FORD MUSEUM
Oakwood, Blvd.
Dearborn, MI 48121
Collections: 100 historical structures, complete with the furnishings and tools of their periods, are on display at Greenfield Village. This is a fine place to see a broad range of American decorative arts, crafts, domestic and industrial tools. Many educational programs are offered.

BAKER FURNITURE MUSEUM
E. Sixth St.
Holland, MI 49423
Collections: 17th through 19th cent. furniture from Europe and the Orient; decorative arts, antique tools, hardware, carvings, and books. This museum is especially valuable for the collector because he can get close to the furniture, which is in the rough.

MICHIGAN SHOWS

MICHIGAN ANTIQUES SHOW
University of Michigan
Crisler Arena
Main St. and Stadium Blvd.
Ann Arbor, MI
Early April
Information: Fred and Margaret Brusher, Mgrs. (305) 781-0608. Co-sponsored by the Univ. of Michigan and the M Club. A new, well regarded show.

THE ANTIQUES MARKET
5055 Saline-Ann Arbor Rd.
Ann Arbor, MI
Third Sunday of each month, 8 to 5.
Information: Fred and Margaret Brusher, Mgrs. (305) 781-0608.
A good flea market.

EAST ROTARY ANTIQUES SHOW
2211 Lake Drive, S. E.
Grand Rapids, MI 49506
April
Information: Call or write the East Rotary Organization at the
above address.

UNIVERSITY-LIGGETT ANTIQUES SHOW
University-Liggett School
850 Braircliff Dr.
Grosse Point Woods, MI 48236
Second week in June.
Information: Call or write the school, Russell Carrell. Mgr.
This is a top Midwest show featuring 18th and 19th cent.
antiques.

ANTIQUES FAIR
County Service Building
2900 Lake St.
Kalamazoo, MI 49001
Early October
Information: Contact the sponsor, the Service Club of
Kalamazoo, at the address above.

MICHIGAN SHOPS

MAZE POTTINGER ANTIQUES
726 N. Woodward Ave.
Birmingham, MI 48011
(313) 646-1996
Maze Pottinger
Hours: 10 to 5:30.
Eighteenth and nineteenth cent. American and English
furniture; brass, some accessories.

THE WOODEN PEG
14 N. Main St.

Clarkston, MI 48016
(313) 652-1749
Fontie M. ApMadoc
Hours: By appointment or chance.
Country furniture; Gaudy Welch, Gaudy Ironstone, soft-paste
porcelain, dated white ironstone, treenware; iron and tin.

COLLECTOR'S CHOICE
444 W. Margaret
Detroit, MI 48203
(Mail address only)
(313) TO9-9186
Bruce Summerville
Hours: By appointment and shows only.
Late 18th and early 19th cent. furniture and accessories.
A dealer of taste and reliability.

WILFRED THOMPSON ANTIQUES
18104 Mt. Elliott
Detroit, MI 48234
(313) 891-7351
Wilfred Thompson
Hours: By appointment.
Early photography; American Indian rugs, baskets, pottery;
general line of American glass and china.

W. RUSSELL BUTTON GALLERY
955 Center St.
Douglas, MI 49406
(616) 857-2194
Mildred Berggren and Randolph Leuser
Hours: 10 to 5 Mon. through Sat., Sun. by appointment.
Antiques, paintings, prints, etchings, watercolors, art objects.
Restoration of oil paintings. The owners are carrying on the
Russell Button tradition.

WASHINGTON STREET ANTIQUES
110 Washington St.
Grand Haven, MI 49417
(616) 842-9340
John Verdon
Hours: 10 to 5 Tues. through Sat. (May through Dec.)
1 to 5 Mon., Wed., Sat. (Jan — April).
Fine English and American furniture; primitives; porcelain
and silver.

THE SIGN OF THE PEACOCK
202 South Bridge
Grand Ledge, MI 48837
(517) 627-7722
Angus B. Cory
Hours: 10 to 5 Tues. through Sat.
General line; ceramic tiles, blue and white porcelain and
pottery, American glass, jewelry. Orientalia, prints, primitives,
bottles, and tins. NADA.

SALLY THOMAS AND COMPANY
Box 277, 3568 Hartland Rd.
Hartland, MI 48029
(313) 632-7358
Sally Thomas
Hours: By chance or appointment.
Period and country furniture, stoneware, treenware, textiles,
spongeware, stick spatter, folk art and metals.

DES ROSS ANTIQUES
Hastings, MI 49058
(616) 945-3816
Des Ross
Hours: By appointment.
Eighteenth and nineteenth cent. furniture and accessories.

MARY MIDDLEBROOK ANTIQUES
7516 E. Michigan Ave.
Jackson, MI 49201
(517) 764-3635
Mary Middlebrook
Hours: By chance or appointment.
General line, primitives, dolls, jewelry, furniture, china, glass,
etc.

WILLIAM LESTERHOUSE ANTIQUES
112 Front St.
Mattawan, MI 49071
(616) 668-3229
Hours: 12 to 5 Wed. through Sun.
American antiques from 1770 to 1870, furniture and accessories;
Windsor chairs, quilts, cherry furniture; postcards, toys, and
general line.

ANN THATCHER ANTIQUES
2400 Mann Rd.
Pontiac, MI 43055
(313) 674-4242
Ann Thatcher
Hours: Tues., Wed., Thurs., Sat.
Country furnishings, primarily 19th cent.

THE SHOP OF ANTIQUITY
7766 Highland Rd. (M59)
Pontiac, MI 48054
(313) 666-2333
Charles E. James
Hours: 10 to 5 Tues. through Sun.
Primitives and country furniture; general line.

VILLAGE GREEN ANTIQUES
P.O. Box 158
Richland, MI 49083
(616) 629-4268
Bernard G. Plomp
Hours: By chance or appointment.
Period furniture and accessories of unusually good quality.

MILDRED FRIEDMAN
300 S. Main
Royal Oak, MI 48067
(313) 399-5358
Hours: By appointment.
Seventeenth and eighteenth cent. English and French provincial furnishings; early Chinese porcelains and pottery; French faience; Georgian lighting; early coromandal screens.

LEONARD BERRY ANTIQUES
520 S. Washington
Royal Oak, MI 48067
(313) 547-0560
Leonard Berry
Hours: 11 to 5 daily, closed Sun.
Eighteenth and nineteenth cent. English and American furniture and accessories.

YE OLD CURIOSITY SHOPPE
3720 Red Arrow Hwy.

St. Joseph, MI 49085
(616) 429-5321
Hours: By appointment.
Old, rare, and out of print books; photographica; marbles.

GOTHIC COTTAGE
3442 Holland Rd.
Saugatuck, MI 49453
(616) 857-2908
John and Laurene Schaberg
Hours: 10 to 5 every day except Mon.
Eighteenth and nineteenth cent. furniture; oriental rugs and
porcelains.

MICHIGAN AUCTIONS

DU MOUCHELLE ART GALLERIES CO.
409 E. Jefferson
Detroit, MI 48226
(313) 963-6255

HAROLD COLE AUCTIONEER
8040 Corunna Rd.
Flint, MI 48504
(313) 635-4449

MINNESOTA

MINNESOTA MUSEUMS

THE MINNEAPOLIS INSTITUTE OF ARTS
201 E. 24th St.
Minneapolis, MN 55404

Collections: European and American paintings and sculpture. Decorative arts and period rooms.

UNIVERSITY GALLERY
University of Minnesota
316 Northrop Memorial Auditorium
Minneapolis, MN 55455
Collections: 20th cent. American art; 18th cent. paintings, prints, and decorative arts.

MINNESOTA SHOWS

HOPKINS HOUSE ANTIQUE SHOW
Hwy. 7
Hopkins, MN 55313
Three times during the year.
Information: Contact Alex M. Wilson, Mgr., 9901 Lyndale Ave., South, Bloomington, MN 55420. (612) 888-2969.

MINNESOTA ANTIQUE DEALERS ASSOCIATION SHOW
Minneapolis Institute of Arts
2400 Third Ave., South
Minneapolis, MN 55404
Mid-May
Information: Call or write Bill Warner, Minneapolis Institute of Arts (612) 870-3175.

KENWOOD ANTIQUE SHOW
Minnesota Church Center
122 Franklin Ave., West
Minneapolis, MN 55404
Fall
Information: Contact Robert A. Luartes, 2504 West Lake of the Isles Blvd., Minneapolis, MN 55405 (612) 374-2641.
Sponsored by the Trinity Community Church.

MOUNT OLIVET ANTIQUE SHOW
Mount Olivet Lutheran Church
15th St. at Knox Ave., South
Minneapolis, MN 55410
Fall
Information: Contact Mrs. R. Beiswanger at the church.

MINNESOTA SHOPS

WENDELL'S ANTIQUES
Box 189, 18 E. Main St.
Dodge Center, MN 55927
(507) 374-2140
Wendell R. Nelson
Hours: 9:30 to 5:30 daily, 2 to 5 Sun.
General line of select antiques. MADA.

LE DUC MANSION
Hastings, MN 55033
(612) 437-4052
C. B. Simmons
Hours: By appointment.
American period furniture; Windsor chairs, highboys, chests,
tables; pieces in curly and tiger maples. Emphasis on 18th cent.
The oldest antique shop in the area.

HUNGRY POINT FARM
R.F.D. 1 (One mile S. of Etter)
Hastings, MN 55033
(612) 437-6574
James and Audrey Meyer
Hours: By appointment only.
Eighteenth and nineteenth cent. American country furniutre;
folk art.

LAMB-TIQUES
117 E. 5th St.
Hastings, MN 55033
(612) 437-9697
Sally Lamb
Hours: 9 to 5 seven days a week.
General line, furniture, depression glass, china.

THE WAGGIN' WHEELER ANTIQUES
Rt. 1, Box 132
Maple Plain, MN 55359
(612) 479-2521
Rita and Roger Wheeler
Hours: Tues. through Sat. by chance or appointment.
Americana, country and period; primitives; general line. MADA.

ROBERT J. RIESBERG
1349 Delaware Ave.
St. Paul (Mendota Heights), MN 55118
(612) 457-1772
Robert J. Riesberg
Hours: By appointment only.
American 18th and early 19th cent. antiques.

TEMPLE'S ANTIQUES
6721 Portland Ave., South
Minneapolis, MN 55423
(612) 861-4025
Joanne M. Koehn
Hours: 10 to 4 Tues. through Sat.
Art glass, dolls, jewelry.

ATHENA ANTIQUES
3907 W. 50th St. Ct.
Minneapolis, (Edina), MN 55424
(612) 374-2641
Elaine and Bob Luartes
Hours: 11:30 to 5:30 daily except Sun.
General line, with fine jewelry a specialty. NADA, MADA.

HUDGINS GALLERY
5026 France Ave.
Minneapolis (Edina), MN 55424
(612) 925-1295
Charles J. Hudgins
Hours: 12 to 4 Tues. through Sat.
Continental, American, Oriental furniture; bronze, porcelain,
prints, paintings, silver. MADA.

POTPOURRI ANTIQUES
7750 Normandale Rd.
Minneapolis (Edina), MN 55435
(612) 835-3430
Helen Le Grand
Hours: 9:30 to 5:30 except Sun.
Furniture, glass, silver, painting and accessories, American
and imported. MADA.

DAVID M. CAFFES ANTIQUES
1901 Bamber Valley Rd., S.W.
Rochester, MN 55901

(507) 282-8497
David M. Caffes
Hours: Seven days a week.
American country furniture; Norwegian items and folk art.

FARR'S LAMP SHOP
27175 Beverly Dr.
Shorewood (Excelsior), MN 55331
(612) 474-8220
Roy and Grace Farr
Hours: Anytime by appointment.
Specializing in kerosene lamps (old and new), shades,
chimneys, wicks, parts. 200 old lamps in stock.

KELJIK ORIENTAL RUGS
1089 Grand Ave.
St. Paul, MN 55105
(612) 222-1197
Var K. Keljik
Hours: 10 to 5 weekdays, 10 to 1 Sat.
Antique Oriental rugs; Continental and Oriental antiques;
lamps.

JOAN L. THAYER
12 Evergreen Rd.
St. Paul, MN 55110
(612) 484-2664
Hours: By appointment only.
Eighteenth and early nineteenth cent. antiques; antique doll
house furnishings; folk art.

THE CORNER DOOR
18344 Minetonka Blvd.
Wayzata, MN 55391
(612) 473-2274
June Webster, Marilyn Hunt, Betsy Freeman, and Dee Savage
Hours: 10 to 4:30 Mon. through Sat.
Antiques and used furniture. Appraisals, house and estate sales.
MADA.

GOLD MINE ANTIQUES
332 S. Broadway
Wayzata, MN 55391
(612) 473-7719
Mary Lou Jensen

Hours: 10 to 4:30 daily except Sun.
Large general line of antiques. MADA.

SARAH HUNT ANTIQUES
6 Old Deer Field Rd.
Welch, MN 55089
(612) 388-3997
Dave and Holly Wesley
Hours: By appointment only.
Eighteenth and nineteenth cent. furniture and accessories.

COBBLESTONE ANTIQUES
1692 Charlton St.
West St. Paul, MN 55118
(612) 451-1175
Mr. and Mrs. Harry Johannsen
Hours: By appointment.
Eighteenth and nineteenth cent. American furniture; painted
furniture and accessories; folk art.

MINNESOTA AUCTIONS

CENTRAL AUCTION HOUSE
Charles Weinberger
4020 Central Ave., N.E.
Columbia Heights, MN 55421
(612) 781-0300

WALLY LAUMEYER
7306 Cleve Ave., East
Inver Grove Heights, MN 55075
(612) 455-9547

J. A. SUNDBERG AUCTIONEER
113 N. First St.
Minneapolis, MN 55401
(612) 332-5993
Antique auctions held on a regular basis.

RADDE BROS. AUCTIONEERS
Watertown, MN 55388
(612) 955-1587

OHIO

OHIO MUSEUMS

CINCINNATI ART MUSEUM
Eden Park
Cincinnati, Ohio 45202
Collections: 15th — 20th cent. European and American art.
Decorative arts.
29,500-volume art library.

CLEVELAND MUSEUM OF ART
11150 East Blvd.
Cleveland, Ohio 44106
Collections: Painting, sculpture, graphics, decorative arts,
and textiles.
78,000-volume library of art books and periodicals, etc.

COLUMBUS GALLERY OF FINE ARTS
480 E. Broad St.
Columbus, Ohio 43215
Collections: Decorative arts, Staffordshire china. The museum
is housed in the Francis C. Sessions Home.

DAYTON ART INSTITUTE
Forest and Riverview Aves.
Dayton, Ohio 45401
Collections: European and American paintings and sculpture.
Prints, ceramics and decorative arts.
20,000-volume art library.

TOLEDO MUSEUM OF ART
2445 Monroe St.
P.O. Box 1013
Toledo, Ohio 45697
Collections: European and American painting and decorative
art.
29,000-volume library of books, slides, and periodicals.

OHIO SHOWS

CINCINNATI ANTIQUES FESTIVAL
Carousel Inn
8001 Reading Road
Cincinnati, Ohio
October
Information: Russell Carrell, Mgr., Salisbury, Connecticut 06068.

GREATER CINCINNATI ANTIQUES SHOW
Convention Center
5th and Elm Sts.
Cincinnati, Ohio
Spring and Fall
Information: Ronald Cox, Mgr., 9480 E. Washington St.,
Indianapolis, IN 46229. (317) 898-8561.

WESTERN RESERVE ANTIQUES SHOW IN CLEVELAND
Crawford Auto Museum
5 East Blvd.
Cleveland, Ohio
Late October
Information: Womens Advisory Council of Western Reserve
Historical Society; or Russell Carrell, Salisbury, Connecticut
06068.

DUNHAM TAVERN MUSEUM ANTIQUES SHOW
Holiday Inn
Rockside Rd.
Cleveland, Ohio
May
Information: Call or write Pappabello Antiques, 12119-23
Lorain Ave., Cleveland, Ohio 44111; or call (216) 226-0355.

THE CHILDHOOD LEAGUE ANTIQUES SHOW
The Imperial House / Arlington Arms
1335 Dublin Rd.
May
Information: Write to N. Pendergast Jones, Mgr., Box 228,
Stonington, Connecticut 06378.

CRUTCHER DAYTON SHOW
Fairgrounds Coliseum
1043 S. Main St. (Rt. 48)

Dayton, Ohio
March
Information: (See listings of Indianapolis Crutcher shows).
This new Crutcher show is one with fine early antiques. Not
the same dealers that exhibit in her Indianapolis and Lebanan,
Ohio shows.

THE GREATER AKRON-CLEVELAND ANTIQUE SHOW
Holiday Inn
Ohio Turnpike Exit 12 at Rt. 8
Hudson, Ohio
Late January
Information: Call or write Adda Brick, Mgr., 27 West Main St.,
Canfield, Ohio 44406; or call (216) 533-5661.

WARREN COUNTY HISTORICAL SOCIETY MUSEUM SHOW
Warren County Fair Grounds
Just north of town on Route 48
Lebanon, Ohio
September and May.
Information: For exact date of show, write Jean Crutcher, Mgr.,
Rt. 1, 7370 Old National Trail East, New Carlisle, Ohio 45344.
A great American show of early antiques.

MEDINA OHIO ANTIQUES SHOW
Holiday Inn
Junction of Interstate 71 and 18
Medina, Ohio
Spring and Fall
Information: H. Allen Wainwright, Mgr., 529 S. Court St.,
Medina, Ohio 44256.

NEW ENGLAND SAMPLER ANTIQUES SHOW
Wagner's Country Inn
Westlake, Ohio
February
Information: The Bay Women's Club, Westlake, Ohio 44145.

GENERAL BREIGHTLER ARMORY HISTORICAL SOCIETY SHOW
Worthington, Ohio 43085
March
Information: Call or write above address, to the attention of
Jack Frost, Mgr.

OHIO SHOPS

ANTIQUES AMERICA
Rt. 177 (19 miles south of Richmond, Indiana)
Camden (Fairhaven), Ohio 45311
(513) 796-3183
Raeburn Stanley and Lawrence E. King
Hours: By appointment.
Fine Americana: Furniture, ceramics, glass, metals, folk art.
Always much historical china.

DAVIDSON'S ANTIQUES
RR 2
Camden (Fairhaven), Ohio 45311
(513) 796-3101
William Davidson
Hours: Sun., otherwise by chance or appointment.
Rural furniture, lacy iron, tin, woodworking tools and
accessories.

MARY JANE'S DOLLS
9318 Wilson Mills Rd.
Chesterland, Ohio 44026
(216) 729-7179
Mr. and Mrs. Donald Poley
Hours: By appointment.
Antique dolls, dollhouses, and furniture and collectible dolls.

CARRIAGE HOUSE ANTIQUES
2306 Upland Place
Cincinnati, Ohio 45206
(513) 281-4161
George Brooks
Hours: 12 to 5 on Sat. and Sun., or by appointment.
Primitives and country items and accessories; some very rare
tins and toys. Their motto is, "Always the unusual."

CREEKWOOD ANTIQUES, INC.
9257 Montgomery Rd. (At Cross County Hwy. exit 14)
Cincinnati, Ohio 45242
(513) 791-8459
Morris and Betty Mason
Hours: 9 to 5:30 Mon. through Sat.
Fine American 17th and 18th cent. formal and country

furniture; early 19th cent. furniture; fine period accessories, primitives of period and quality, paintings, weathervanes, tole, chalk, pewter, redware, woodenware, and clocks.

WILMAR ANTIQUES
3318 Erie at Victoria
Cincinnati, Ohio 45208
(513) 961-6358
M. E. Oshry and W. J. Baude
Hours: 11 to 4 Tues. — Sat.
Eighteenth and early nineteenth cent. English and American furniture and accessories, prints and other decorative furnishings.

STAN NELSON ANTIQUES
Cincinnati, Ohio 45209
(513) 731-2215 or 731-8483
Stanley F. Nelson
Hours: By appointment only.
Brilliant period cut glass, fine porcelains, silver, orientals, and other objects d'art. NADA.

BERGMAN'S ANTIQUES
12401 Woodland Ave.
Cleveland, Ohio 44120
(216) 791-6418
Bill Bergman
Hours: 10 to 5:15.
Eighteenth and nineteenth cent. European and Oriental china, objects d'art; early quality period furniture; ivories, jades and enamels; paintings, bronzes and quality antique jewelry. NADA.

PAPPABELLO ANTIQUES
12119-23 Lorain Ave.
Cleveland, Ohio 44111
(216) 226-0355
Jas. Pappas and Robert Ciancibello
Hours: 10:30 to 4:30 daily.
Art and cut glass; Oriental rugs, Orientalia; 19th and 20th cent. American, English and French furniture; Wedgwood. NADA.

WOODRINGS ANTIQUES
Route 250
Colerain, Ohio 43916
Jane and Bill Woodring

Hours: 10 to 5 daily, closed Wed.
General line of furniture in the rough and refinished, accessories.

TREASURE TROVE ANTIQUES
2893 North High St.
Columbus, Ohio 43202
(614) 261-8886
Toni Alexander
Hours: 11 to 7 daily, closed Mon.
Eighteenth cent. to early twentieth cent. English porcelain, nineteenth cent. silver. NADA.

TOWPATH ANTIQUES
3838 Indian Ripple Rd.
Dayton, Ohio 45440
(513) 426-6760
Mrs. Laurel A. Cox
Hours: 9 to 5 daily.
Authentic cast iron toys and banks, pattern glass, iron, brass, copper and wood primitives, stoneware, old advertising items.

MRS. MYRTLE W. AMICK
Delaware, Ohio
(614) 369-3975
MRS. OPAL M. SMITH
Columbus, Ohio
(614) 267-1382
Hours: At shows or by appointment only.
Country antiques, restored and refinished; accessories.
Everything guaranteed.

DRUMMER BOY ANTIQUES
325 S. High St.
Dublin, Ohio 43017
(614) 889-2230 or 451-9268
Virginia W. Kempton
Hours: 11 to 4:30.
Formal and country furniture of the 18th and 19th cent.; quilts, coverlets, soft paste, paintings, pottery, iron, tin, and pewter.

ALLAN J. HODGES ANTIQUES
12700 Lake Avenue
Lakewood, Ohio 44107

(216) 521-5060
Allan J. Hodges
Hours: By appointment only, and shows.
Rare American glassware, blown, pressed, and early cut; cup
plates and early glass lighting.

GAZING BALL
Lyndhurst, Ohio 44124
(216) 382-0163
Jackie Olson
Hours: By appointment only.
Early toys, samplers, quilts, coverlets. Stevensgraphs and
related stitchery; early flint and pattern glass; jewelry,
sterling souvenir spoons, small pieces of silver; early pottery
and early ironstone; small furniture, children's books,
valentines.

OHIO BOOKHUNTER
323 Park Avenue West
Mansfield, Ohio 44907
(419) 756-0655
J. Stark
Hours: By appointment only.
Rare books, manuscripts, fine books, first editions,
collector's stock, general stock.

H. ALAN WAINWRIGHT
529 S. Court St.
Medina, Ohio 44256
(216) 725-6249
H. Alan Wainwright
Hours: By appointment only.
Early American furniture, accessories, folk art, etc.

BROCKHAVEN ANTIQUES
3700 Grand Avenue
Middletown, Ohio 45042
(513) 422-3036
Mrs. B. E. Brock
Hours: By appointment and mail order.
Specializing in old French Haviland; also general line.

JOAN R. COULTER
123 Center St.
P.O. Box 356

Milan, Ohio 44846
(419) 499-4061
Hours: Telephone for appointment.
American antiques.

CRAWFORD AND DELO ANTIQUES
853 Vienna Ave.
Niles, Ohio 44446
(216) 544-3842
S. L. Crawford and J. E. Delo
Hours: By appointment only.
American and English 18th and 19th cent. country and formal
furniture; brass, copper, paintings, prints, glass, small
wooden wares; general line.

YANKEE TRADER ANTIQUES
4050 Broadview Rd.
Richfield, Ohio 44286
(216) 659-3501
Peg Sidaway
Hours: By chance or appointment.
Country, Victorian and period furniture and accessories;
dolls, children's furniture and banks.

MAURICE G. MAGILL ANTIQUES
5140 Morris Road
Springfield, Ohio 45502
(513) 399-2261
Maurice G. Magill
Hours: By appointment.
American country furniture and decorative accessories of the
period.

LARRY MELVIN ANTIQUES
128 Bellevue Ave.
Springfield, Ohio 45503
(513) 323-4296
Judy Melvin
Hours: 10 to 4 or by appointment.
Early Pennsylvania and Ohio furniture; primitives and early
tools.

McILWAIN ANTIQUES
5694 Main St.
Sylvania, Ohio 43560

(419) 882-1636
Lionel and Coral McIlwain
Hours: 1 to 5 Mon. through Sat.
Victorian and country furniture; primitives, glass and china.

WAYNE SIDDENS AND BOB VALENTINE ANTIQUES
5270 West Alexis Rd.
Sylvania, Ohio 43560
(419) 882-1557 and 882-1249
Wayne Siddens and Bob Valentine
Hours: 11 to 5:30 Mon. through Sat.
General line; 18th cent. American furniture, Victorian and
country furniture; cut and art glass, silver, Oriental rugs, and
paintings. NADA.

CUSTER ANTIQUES AND INVESTMENT
4139 Monroe St.
Toledo, Ohio 43606
(419) 472-0050
Richard Bohl
Hours: 10 to 5:30 weekdays; 11 to 4 Sat., Sept. through May.
Or by appointment.
The usual in fine art glass, oils, bronzes, Tiffany lamps,
porcelains, ivories, Orientals, clocks, and furniture.
Specializing in watches.

JIM De CURTINS
5325 Horseshoe Bend Rd.
Troy, Ohio 45373
(New telephone number not yet available.)
Hours: By chance or appointment.
Eighteenth and nineteenth century country furniture and
accessories, painted furniture and "reproduction tin";
specializing in lighting devices. Mr. De Curtins is a tinsmith.
This type of craftsmanship is rare today, especially when
combined with a knowledge of antiques.

ROBERT D. LEATH ANTIQUES
323 E. Main St.
Troy, Ohio 45373
(513) 335-1763
Robert D. Leath
Hours: By appointment only.
Eighteenth and early nineteenth cent. furniture and accessories.

Many items for restorations (early locks, hardware, fireplace equipment, etc.).

NELLIE MAY MILLIGAN ANTIQUES
110 E. Court St.
Urbana, Ohio 43078
(513) 652-1567
Nellie May Milligan
Hours: 10 to 4 or by appointment. Also shows.
Eighteenth and nineteenth cent. American and English furniture and accessories (Ohio, Pa. and N.E. primitive and period). Mostly as found, some refinished. Ohio representative for old fashioned milk paint, spatterware, pewter.
No Victorian or oak.

BAKER'S ANTIQUES OF WASHINGTON SQUARE
Waynesville, Ohio 45068
Shop: (513) 897-6552; residence: (513) 298-2077
Robert J. and Katherine N. Baker
Hours: 12 to 5:30 Sat. and Sun.; otherwise by chance or appointment.
Furniture, china, glass, primitives, accessories.

OHIO AUCTIONS

GARTH'S AUCTIONS, INC.
2690 Stratford Rd.
Delaware, Ohio 43015
(614) 362-4771

DAVE KESSLER, AUCTIONEER
New Paris, Ohio 45347
(513) 437-7071

TRADE WINDS AUCTION GALLERY
Citizens Bank Bldg.
Wadsworth, Ohio 44281
(216) 336-3911

WISCONSIN

WISCONSIN MUSEUMS

VILLA TERRACE MUSEUM OF DECORATIVE ARTS
2220 N. Villa Terrace Ave.
Milwaukee, WI
Collections: Decorative arts of all periods; a good library of art reference books. This is a branch of the Milwaukee Art Center.

CHARLES ALLIS ART LIBRARY
1630 E. Royal Pl.
Milwaukee, WI 53202
Collections: An art museum housed in a 1908 Tudor style house. Chinese porcelains, Han through Ch'ing dynasties; French antiques; decorative arts.

ELVEHJEM ART CENTER
University of Wisconsin
800 University Ave.
Madison, WI 53706
Collections: Paintings, sculpture, graphics, decorative arts. A 65,000 volume library of art books.

STATE HISTORICAL SOCIETY OF WISCONSIN
816 State St.
Madison, WI 53706
Collections: Dolls, Civil War items, costumes, coins, stamps, decorative arts, glass and ceramics.

THE BERGSTROM ART CENTER AND MUSEUM
165 N. Park Ave.
Neenah, WI 54956
Collections: Antique and modern glass paperweights; German glass; American paintings, sculpture and graphics; American Victorian glass baskets; Tiffany, glass bottles, lustre; decorative arts. A 600 volume art and antiques library.

MINERAL POINT, WISCONSIN 53565
This is an historic town that has been restored by its residents and the State Historical Society of Wisconsin. There are many dealers here and in the nearby towns. The houses are built in

various historical styles,with the emphasis on Greek Revival and Victorian.

VILLA LOUIS AND MUSEUM
Villa Rd. and Boilvin
Prairie du Chien, WI 53821
Collections: The Villa Louis was the home of fur trader Hercules Dousman. The house was built in 1843, and contains the Dousman family collection and a 3,500 volume historical library.

WISCONSIN SHOWS

ST. MONICA ANTIQUE SHOW
Milwaukee (Whitefish Bay), WI
Close to St. Valentine's Day
Information: Inquire of Mary Boulet, Mgr., 6043 North Lake Dr., Milwaukee, WI 43217

THE MILWAUKEE ART CENTER ANTIQUES SHOW
Milwaukee Art Center
750 N. Lincoln Memorial Dr.
Milwaukee, WI 53202
Second week in November.
Information: Call or write the Art Center. An excellent show.

MINERAL POINT ANTIQUE SHOW
Fair Grounds (US 151)
Mineral Point, WI
Second weekends in June and October.
Information: Ray Prasch, Mgr., 150 High St., Mineral Point, WI 53565.

WISCONSIN SHOPS

LANTERN BOOKSHOP
942 Wisconsin Ave.
Beloit, WI 53511
(608) 362-4740
Marlowe Rund
Hours: By appointment.
New, old, rare, and out of print books. Free search service.

ARVILLA'S ANTIQUE SHOPPE
Boulder Junction, WI 54521
(715) 385-2143
Arvilla Doss
Hours: 10 to 5, June through Sept.
Country pine furniture and accessories. NADA.

RED BARN ANTIQUES
Hwy. 42
Ephraim, WI 54211
(414) 854-2045
Misses Binder, McAghon, Wright
Hours: 10 to 5, May through Oct.
Primitives, glass, china, furniture, books, postcards. NADA.

LIL GAROT ANTIQUES
1276 Velp Ave.
Greenbay, WI 54303
(414) 499-2202
Lyllyanne Garot
Hours: 9 to 12, weekdays only.
China, glass, furniture, Art Deco, valentines, fans, postcards.

PARASOL ANTIQUES
1346 Friess Lake Rd.
Hubertus (Holly Hill area) WI 53033
(Call Hubertus info. for telephone number.)
Carmen Kraft Slater
Hours: By chance or appointment.
Glass, china, silver, jewelry, primitives, collectibles.

JAEGER ANTIQUES
459 S. Randall Ave.
Janesville, WI 53545
(608) 754-8585
Josephine E. Jaeger
Hours: Wed. through Sun., afternoons only.
Furniture over 100 years old; cut glass, lamps, brass,
copper. NADA.

CENTURY FARM ANTIQUES
5331 Cemetery Rd. (Rt. 5)
Janesville, WI 53545
(608) 752-0092
Dorothy Risch and Charles Risch

Hours: 10:30 to 5:30 Mon. through Sat., 1 to 5:30 Sun.
Country furniture, primitives, glass, china, general line.
Furniture refinished by owner's son. NADA.

KING GEORGE
Madison, WI 53711
(608) 271-2348
Gordon and Marjorie Davenport
Hours: By appointment only.
Selected fine antiques and period furniture. NADA.

AMERICAN ANTIQUES AND APPRAISAL
505 Commercial St. (Hwy. 14)
Mazomanie, WI 53560
(608) 767-2608
Karen and Richard Rahn
Hours: 10 to 5 Sat. ; 11 to 5 Sun.; weekdays by chance or
appointment.
Period furniture; oak in rough and finished; lamps, china, glass,
silver, quilts, general line.

MARSHALL R. BERKOFF
9079 N. Tennyson Dr.
Milwaukee, WI 53217
(414) 352-2942
Marshall R. Berkoff
Hours: By appointment.
Currier and Ives, other original lithographs.

GABRIEL RUG CO. INC.
420 E. Wells St.
Milwaukee, WI 53202
(414) 276-2840
Lee N. Gabriel
Hours: 9 to 5 weekdays, 9 to 4 Sat.
Oriental rugs: Persian, Chinese, Caucasian, Turkish, and
Turkoman.

LENZ GALLERY
7733 W. Burleigh
Milwaukee, WI 53222
(414) 444-5375
Thomas E. Lenz
Hours: 10 to 5 Tues. through Sat.
Fine 18th and 19th cent. paintings, American and European.

NEY-LONDES, THE ANTIQUE ARTS
610 E. Mason
Milwaukee, WI 53202
(414) 272-6300
Mary Londes Naparstek
Hours: 10:30 to 5 Mon. through Sat.; appointments advisable.
Period English and American furniture; paintings, prints and
drawings; quality English and Oriental porcelains; brass and
pewter; American glass. Seventeenth cent. through early
nineteenth cent. only.

VERONA SUNVOLD
2867 N. Marietta Ave.
Milwaukee, WI 53211
(414) 962-2566
Verona Sunvold
Hours: By appointment.
American antiques; custom made lamps and shades.
Mrs. Sunvold is an expert cabinet maker and designer.

VILLAGE ANTIQUE CENTER
1800 E. Capitol Dr.
Milwaukee, WI 53211
(414) 332-8484
Arnold Prochep, Mgr.
Hours: 10:30 to 5 Mon. through Sat.
The center houses 90 dealers in 12 rooms.

WHITE SHUTTERS ANTIQUES SHOP
771 N. Jefferson St.
Milwaukee, WI 53202
(414) 271-8866
Dorothy M. Taylor
Hours: 11 to 5 Mon. through Sat.
General line; art, pressed and cut glass; china, silver, lamps,
toys, dolls, picture frames, brass. NADA.

THE PICK ANTIQUES
150 High St.
Mineral Point, WI 53565
(608) 987-2877
Ray Prasch
Hours: Appointment suggested.
Mostly pre 1850 antiques: sandwich glass and blown flint

glass; English porcelains; country furniture with original paint; accessories of the period.

JEAN LINEWEBER
5216 Mesa Rd.
Monona, WI 53716
(608) 222-3787
Jean Lineweber
Hours: By appointment only.
Americana, 18th and 19th cent.; country furniture and accessories; pottery, iron, tin, copper, brass, drawings, prints, paintings, firearms, quilts, coverlets.

FLORENTINE ANTIQUES
18715 W. Greenfield Ave.
New Berlin, WI 53151
(414) 782-5080
Florentine Ruck
Hours: By chance or appointment.
English and American furniture of 17th and 18th cent.; copper, brass, china; primitives.

FRIGHTENED HARE ANTIQUES
1557 S. Greenbay Rd. (Hwy. 31)
Racine, WI 53406
(414) 633-7035
Terry and Angela Brinton
Hours: By appointment.
Country furniture, lamps and accessories.

WHITEHOUSE FARM ANTIQUES
P.O. Box 242
Shawano, WI 54166
(414) 524-4421
Doreen Mathie
Hours: 10 to 5 Mon. through Sat.; 1 to 4 Sun.
General line; primitives, some in the rough.

MEADOWCREST ANTIQUES
P.O. Box 288
Shawano, WI 54166
(715) 526-2210
Jacob J. Klein
Hours: By appointment daily.

General line; china, French cameo glass, cut glass, American silver, paper collectibles, buttons. Everything guaranteed. NADA. WADA.

LAURETTA'S ANTIQUES
Rt. 2
Tomahawk, WI 54481
(715) 453-3668
Lauretta Shea
Hours: 9 to 5 Mon. through Sat., May through Oct.
Mostly primitive furniture, refinished; art glass.

THE DONALD WM. HALLOCKS
222 Carrington St.
Waupum, WI 53963
(414) 324-2209
Hours: By appointment.
Fine American antiques; pattern glass, primitives, paperweights, silver.

EDMONDS — CLASEN ANTIQUES
Rt. 2 (Hwy. 13), Box 73
Wisconsin Dells, WI 53965
(608) 253-5162
Clara Edmonds and Lucele Clasen
Hours: 9 to 5, seven days a week.
Colored glass, painted china, lamps, cut glass, copper, brass, primitives, wrought iron. NADA.

WISCONSIN AUCTIONS

JACK BARRETT AUCTIONEER
Box 692
Wisconsin Rapids, WI 54494
(715) 423-2252

LESTER BUE AUCTIONEER
2237 Alton Rd. (Rt. 3)
Beloit, WI 53511
(608) 364-4270

HORN AND PAUL AUCTIONEERS
6901 N. River Rd.

West Bend, WI 53095
(414) 334-4466

FOY KNEISEL AUCTIONEER
Friendship, WI 53934
(608) 339-3130

WALTER SCHROEDER AUCTIONEER
Rt. 4, Box 383
Fort Atkinson, WI 53538
(414) 563-9177

A silver tablespoon made by Philip Syng, Jr. (1703–89) for the Logan family of Philadelphia, circa 1730. An intrinsically beautiful object, enriched by its remarkable historical associations, this spoon is a quintessential example of all the reasons why people collect antiques.

Syng was a good friend of Benjamin Franklin, and helped him in many civic affairs, including the founding of the first circulating library in America and the institution that was to become the University of Pennsylvania. A versatile craftsman, Syng even designed machinery for Franklin's electrical experiments. Syng is most famous today for the inkstand he made in 1752 for the Provincial Assembly, which was used in the signing of the Declaration of Independence and the Constitution of the United States.

The spoon was made for the family of James Logan (1674–1751), one of the three or four most important men of his day. A close friend of William Penn, as well as his agent in Pennsylvania, Logan contributed greatly to the success of the Pennsylvania colony. Like Syng, Logan was acquainted with Franklin, and supported much of his work.

The lives of four great Americans from our past — Franklin and Syng, Logan and Penn — are brought together in this simple spoon. Rarely is so much of a nation's history embodied in a single object.

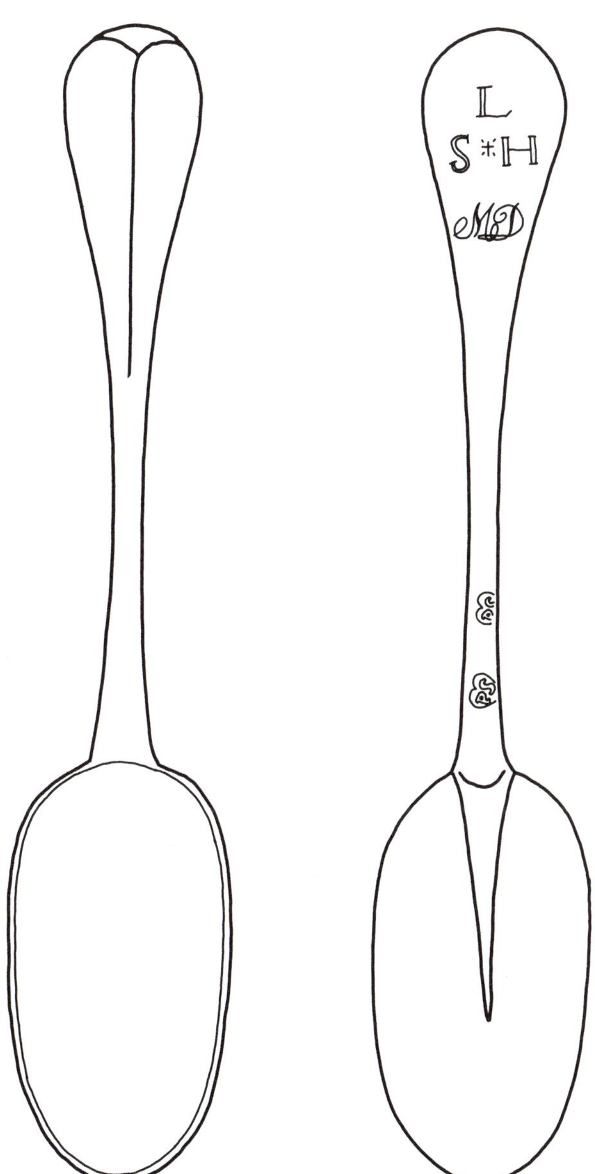

L
S ✻ H
M D

Bibliography

This bibliography has been selected to provide only those books which are excellent and easily available. The few books listed that are out of print usually can be found in a good art library. Of course, we cannot present here all the existing good books on the categories or periods mentioned in this book. But the books listed here should aid you in locating further sources of information inasmuch as most of them contain their own sizable bibliographies on the subjects they discuss.

There are fewer books available for some categories of late nineteenth and early twentieth century collectibles than for earlier periods. Much research is yet to be done in some of these areas, and some that has been done is not yet in book form. Occasionally, however, there are museum exhibition catalogues written about the newer collectibles which can be quite helpful; moreover, articles on these later categories frequently appear in *The Magazine Antiques, The National Antiques Review, Spinning Wheel,* and other periodicals. A reference librarian can help you use cumulative indexes to locate articles on topics of interest. Also, many libraries maintain clipping files on specific subjects.

BIBLIOGRAPHY

GENERAL

Kirk, John T. *The Impecunious Collector's Guide to American Antiques.* New York: Knopf, 1975. Large paperback edition. The subtitle contains the following: "How to Recognize If a Piece is Genuine and Has Permanent Aesthetic Merit." More lessons in aesthetics that can be useful whether or not you have or develop Mr. Kirk's enthusiasm for "deliciously grungy surfaces."

Hume, Ivor Noël. *All the Best Rubbish.* New York: Harper & Row, 1974. "Being an Antiquary's Account of the Pleasures and Perils of Studying and Collecting Everyday Objects from the Past." A sophisticated and historical approach to collecting by the Director of the Department of Archeology at Colonial Williamsburg.

Boger, Louise. *Furniture Past and Present.* New York: Doubleday, 1966. The complete guide to furniture styles from ancient to modern times.

Boger, Louise, and Batterson, H. *The Compilers' and Editors' Dictionary of Antiques and the Decorative Arts.* New York: Charles Scribner's Sons, 1957.

Davidson, Marshall B. (author and editor-in charge). *The American Heritage History of Antiques.* New York: American Heritage. 3 vols. Vol. I, *Colonial Antiques,* 1967; vol. II, *From the Revolution to the Civil War,* 1968; vol. III, *From the Civil War to World War I,* 1969. Remarkable set of books with a splendid historical background.

Stillinger, Elizabeth. *The Antiques Guide to Decorative Arts in America: 1600–1875.* New York: E. P. Dutton, 1972. An important book for anyone interested in any of the many facets of the subject.

Comstock, Helen, ed. *The Concise Encyclopedia of American Antiques.* New York: Hawthorne, 1965. Much reliable information. No date is given on my copy.

Durant, Mary. *The American Heritage Guide to Antiques.* New York: American Heritage, 1970. Very useful illustrated glossary.

Maddan, Betty I. *Art, Crafts, and Architecture in Early Illinois.* Urbana: University of Illinois Press, 1974. Insofar as I know, this is the only such book written about a Midwestern state. It is a very fine book.

Crossman, Carl L. *The China Trade Export Paintings, Furniture, Silver and Other Objects.* Princeton: Pyne Press, 1972. This book deals with Chinese export wares made for use or purchase from Chinese mercantile establishments during the early decades of the United States starting in 1784.

Lipman, Jean. *American Folk Art in Wood, Metal, and Stone.* New York: Dover, 1972. The excellent text is well-illustrated.

Constantino, Ruth T. *How to Know French Antiques.* New York: Clarkson N. Potter, 1961. The illustrations in this book show some of the finest cabinetmaking, silver, ceramics, etc. made in the West. Few of the objects are available in the market. Nonetheless, it is a valuable book containing much excellent advice on the art of collecting.

Oglesby, Catherine. *French Provincial Decorative Art.* New York: Charles Scribner's Sons, 1961. Bonanza Books. Often provincial French antiques can be combined happily with English or American provincial furniture and accessories.

McClinton, Katherine M. *Collecting American Victorian Antiques, Furniture and Decorative Accessories.* New York: Charles Scribner's Sons, 1966.

Selz, Peter, and Constantine, Mildred, eds. *Art Nouveau Art and Design at the Turn of the Century*. New York: Museum of Modern Art. Distributed by New York Graphic Society, Boston, 1959. Rev. ed. 1975.

Barilli, Renato. *Art Nouveau*. London and New York: Hamlyn, 1969 (Cameo series).

Clark, Robert Judson. *The Arts and Crafts Movement in America 1876–1916*. Princeton: Princeton Univ. Press, 1972. Exhibition catalogue for show organized by the Art Museum of Princeton University and The Art Institute of Chicago. Texts by Martin Eidelberg, Davida Hanks, Susan Otis Thompson, and others.

Lesieutre, Alain. *The Spirit and Splendour of Art Deco*. New York: Paddington Press, 1974.

Brunhammer, Yvonne. *The Nineteen Twenties Style*. London and New York: Hamlyn, 1969.

Hillier, Bevis. *The World of Art Deco*. Minneapolis: Minneapolis Institute of Arts, 1971. Exhibition catalogue.

Kovel, Ralph, and Terry. *The Kovels' Complete Antiques Price List*. New York: Crown. This guide to the prices for which a wide range of antiques and collectibles were offered for sale or sold at auction is the best one. Any price guide can give you only a limited idea of what the price represents in the quality and condition of the objects listed. It can help you to know something of the relative costs of objects in various categories. The prices are compiled by computer from June to June, and the book is issued promptly.

FURNITURE

American

Kirk, John T. *Early American Furniture*. New York: Knopf, 1970. Large paperback edition, 1974. The subtitle: "How to Recognize, Evaluate, Buy, and Care for the Most Beautiful Pieces — High-Style, Country, Primitive, and Rustic," is an exact description of the book. The handling of the difficult subject of aesthetics, as applied to this subject, is masterful.

Comstock, Helen. *American Furniture*. New York: Crown, 1962. Bonanza Books. A complete guide to seventeenth, eighteenth, and nineteenth century styles. 700 illustrations. A valuable book for study and reference.

Bjerkoe, Ethal Hall. *The Cabinet-Makers of America*. New York: Doubleday, 1957. Now issued by Bonanza Books. This book is helpful in showing the regional differences in cabinet-making in the colonies and early years of the Republic, as well as the interrelations of styles made by various makers of furniture.

Downs, Joseph. *American Furniture: Queen Anne and Chippendale Periods*. New York: MacMillan, 1952. Illustrated with more than 400 examples from the Winterhus collection. The artistry of the American cabinet-maker has never been shown to better advantage, nor described with more expertise than in this volume. A book for study, reference, and enjoyment.

Montgomery, Charles F. *American Furniture: The Federal Period*. New York: Viking, 1966. Montgomery has done for this period what Joseph Downs did for the Queen Anne-Chippendale periods in American furniture. Another great Winterhus book.

Sack, Albert. *Fine Points of Furniture: Early American*. New York: Crown, 1950. 14th printing, 1971. An illustrated guide to the what and why of quality.

Palmer, Brooks. *The Book of American Clocks*. New York: MacMillan, 1950.

________. *A Treasury of American Clocks.* New York: Mac-Millan, 1967.

Fales, Dean A., Jr. *American Painted Furniture 1660–1880.* New York: E. P. Dutton, 1972. This book shows how paint can give ordinary wood extraordinary charm. Well-deserved mention is given illustrations and design editor Robert Bishop and general editor April I. Nelson.

Otto, Celia Jackson. *American Furniture of the 19th Century.* New York: Viking, 1965.

Marsh, Moreton. *The Easy Expert in Collecting and Restoring American Antiques.* Philadelphia and New York: J. B. Lippincott, 1959. A book that has been through many printings. Much useful information.

Ormsbee, Thomas H. *Field Guide to American Victorian Furniture.* Boston: Little, Brown, 1952. Reissued by Bonanza Books. This is a very helpful book with excellent line drawings and clear text.

Andrews, Edward Deming, and Andrews, Faith. *Shaker Furniture.* New York: Dover. "The Craftsmanship of an American Communal Sect" is well-documented and illustrated.

British

Wills, Geoffrey. *English Furniture 1550–1760.* New York: Doubleday, 1971. English furniture is a large and rewarding category. The collector will want more specialized books if he decides to concentrate on a particular segment of the field.

________. *English Furniture 1760–1900.* Garden City, New York: Doubleday, 1971.

Nickerson, David. *English Furniture of the 18th Century.* Weidenfeld and Nicholson. Also Putnam, New York, 1963

(Pleasures and treasures). An overview of the century of greatest creativity and accomplishment.

Fastnedge, Ralph. *Sheraton Furniture*. London: Faber & Faber, 1962.

Jourdain, Margaret. *Regency Furniture 1795–1820*. London: Country Life. New York: Charles Scribner's Sons.

Cescinsky, Herbert, and Webster, Malcolm R. *English Domestic Clocks*. New York: Bonanza.

Goodison, Nicholas. *English Barometers 1680 1860*. New York: 1968. An exceedingly worthwhile book on the many English forms of this decorative object.

SILVER

American Silver and American Plated Silver

Fales, Martha Gandy. *Early American Silver*. Rev. and enlarged with more illustrations. New York: Dutton, 1973. This large paperback is probably the most helpful single book on the subject, and it is available.

Kauffman, Henry J. *The Colonial Silversmith, His Techniques and His Products*. Camden, N.J.: Thomas Nelson, 1969. This book shows how our first art form was made.

Pleasants, Jacob, and Sill, Howard. *Maryland Silversmiths 1715–1830*. Harrison, New York: R. A. Green, 1972. An unabridged republication of the first edition of 300 copies published in 1930. The reissue of this book is important because much Maryland silver is very fine but it has been neglected. Except for this book, little has been written about the subject until recently.

Buhler, Kathryn C., and Hood, Graham. *American Silver — Garvan and Other Collections in the Yale University Art*

Gallery. New Haven: Yale Univ. Press, 1970. Two large volumes profusely illustrated. This is the best collection of American silver. Referring to these remarkable objects will help a collector to make the best choices in a rare and expensive category.

McClinton, Katherine M. *Collecting American 19th Century Silver*. New York: Charles Scribner's Sons, 1968. A very good book concerned with some of the more available categories of American silver.

Turner, Noel D. *American Silver Flatware 1837–1910*. Cranbury, New Jersey: A. S. Barnes, 1972. Much information is given on late handmade flatware patterns and much more on sterling machine-made flatware. Also pewter Britannia and brass and a large section on electroplate.

Rainwater, Dorothy T. *Encyclopedia of American Silver Manufacturers*. New York: Crown, 1975. Rev. ed. Much interesting information for collectors of American silver made after the mid-19th century, including plated silver.

Schnadig, Victor. *American Victorian Figural Napkin Rings*. Des Moines, Iowa: Wallace-Homestead, 1970. This first and only book on the subject is excellent and complete. Over 700 napkin rings are shown and described. Information is given as to maker, catalogue number, and year of production.

Rainwater, Dorothy T., and Ivan, H. *American Silver Plate*. Hanover, Pa.: Thomas Nelson, 1972. This book will be most helpful in this collectible which includes an amazing diversity of objects and styles.

Kovel, Ralph M., and Terry H. *American Silver, Pewter and Silver Plate*. New York: Crown, 1961. This is a book of marks. As such, it is useful, but more comprehensive than reliable. The book of marks for American silver similar to Sir James Jackson's books on British marks has yet to be written.

British Silver and Sheffield Plate

Taylor, Gerald. *Silver*. First published 1956, reprinted several times. Now a Pelican Original papercover edition. An excellent book on British antique silver.

Wills, Geoffrey. *Silver, For Pleasure and Investment*. New York: Arco, 1969. Well-illustrated guide to 18th century English silver.

Banister, Judith. *English Silver*. New York: Hawthorn, 1966. Judith Banister's books are standard equipment for collectors.

______. *Late Georgian and Regency Silver*. Levittown, New York: Transatlantic Arts, 1971. (Country Life Collectors' guides.)

Jackson, Sir Charles James. *English Goldsmiths and Their Marks*. New York: Dover, 1964. 2nd rev. ed. The most complete book on the subject.

Banister, Judith, ed. *English Silver Hallmarks from circa 1554*. London: W. Foulsham, 1970. With 500 makers' marks from 1697–1900. This helpful book fits easily into pocket or handbag.

Frost, T. W. *The Price Guide to Old Sheffield Plate*, Suffolk, England: Antique Collector's Club, 1971. This book contains much information about old Sheffield plate. The price guide part of the book is secondary to the help it gives in understanding and identifying old Sheffield plate.

CERAMICS

General

Webster, Donald Blake. *Decorated Stoneware Pottery of North America.* Rutland, Vt.: Charles E. Tuttle, 1971. 3rd printing, 1975.

Cushion, J. P., and Honey, W. B. *Handbook of Pottery and Porcelain Marks.* Boston: Boston Book and Art Shop, n.d.

American Ceramics

Guilland, Harold F. *Early American Folk Pottery.* Philadelphia, New York, London: Chilton, 1971.

Barret, Richard Carter. *Bennington Pottery and Porcelain.* New York: Crown, 1958.

Osgood, Cornelius. *The Jug and Related Stoneware of Bennington.* Rutland, Vermont: Charles E. Tuttle, 1971.

Horney, Wayne B. *Pottery of the Galena Area.* East Dubuque, Illinois: Telegraph-Herald Com'l Printing Division.

Altman, Seymour, and Violet. *The Book of Buffalo Pottery.* New York: Bonanza Books, 1973.

Peck, Herbert. *The Book of Rookwood Pottery.* New York: Crown, 1968.

Koval, Ralph, and Terry. *The Koval's Guide to American Art Pottery.* New York: Crown, 1975.

Evans, Paul. *Art Pottery of the United States: An Encyclo-*

pedia of Producers and Their Marks. New York: Charles Scribner's Sons, 1975.

English Pottery and Porcelain

Godden, Geoffrey A. *An IIllustrated Encyclopedia of British Pottery and Porcelain*. New York: Crown, 1966. All the objects shown in this book are marked. This often makes possible the identification of unmarked pieces. Marking was often erratic until the middle of the 19th century, or only the larger pieces such as a tea pot were marked.

Hughes, Barnard, and Therle. *The Collectors Encyclopaedia of English Ceramics*. Abby Library, London — Murray's Sales and Service Co. 146-152. Holloway Road, London, N7, 1968. Much helpful information.

Godden, Geoffrey A. *Caughley and Worchester Porcelains 1775–1800*. New York: Praeger, 1969. This book is important because it contains the information resulting from the excavations of these two factory sites which cleared up some incorrect attributions of long standing. Geoffrey Godden has written several books on other British potters. Look for them if you are interested in Minton, Coalport, etc.

Towner, Donald C. *English Cream-colored Earthenware*. New York: Pittman. A small, splendid book on the remarkably aesthetic creamware of the 18th century, as made and decorated in England. This is an available category.

John, W. D., and Baker, Warren. *Old English Lustre Pottery*. The Ceramic Book Company, 1951. 2nd ed, 1962. Rare and expensive but the definitive book on the subject. Usually available in an art library.

Bedford, John. *Old English Lustre Pottery* (#5 Collector's Pieces series). New York: Walker, 1968. 3rd printing. This book is a resumé of the Old English Lustre Pottery of W. D. John and Wattern Barker. A very useful book.

Whiter, Leonard. *Spode*. New York: Praeger, 1970. This book published in the 200th year of the founding of the factory of Josiah Spode I, is about the early period 1770–1883. The Spodes were great innovators — bone china — a superior stoneware, "new stone"— feldspar porcelain, etc. The first lustre decorated ceramics came from this oven.

Little, W. L. *Staffordshire Blue*. New York: Crown, 1969. This book includes transfer printed earthenware made for foreign markets, including some American scenes, and the domestic trade.

Larsen, Ellouise Baker. *American Historical Views on Staffordshire China. 1939–1950*. New York: Dover, 1975. 3rd. ed. Containing a new supplement of 350 illustrations.

Laidacker, Sam. *Anglo-American China Part I*. Published by author, 1954. 2nd ed.

________. *Anglo-American China Part II*. Published by author, 1951. These two reference books, long out of print, may usually be found in a good art library. They have never been equalled in usefulness in sorting out these large categories. Part I deals with the export ware made with American scenes. Part II with ware, mostly made for export to the former colonies of British scenes. Other types are discussed. Samuel Laidacker is one of the great scholars of Americana. The prices given are obsolete, but they were realistic in their time and now serve to divide the rare from the unrare.

Armin, David, and Linda. *Historical Staffordshire: An Illustrated Checklist*. Danville, Virginia: Arman, 1974. The illustrations in this book are helpful. The arrangement leaves much to be desired. The authors say that the prices listed "are strictly our opinion and our opinion only." This haphazard method of price determination can have little value. However, their definition of condition can be of help — keeping in mind the fact that the more desirable the scene, the more value it has, whether there are evidences of age or not.

Fox, Eleanor J., and Edward G. *Gaudy Dutch*. Pottsville, Pennsylvania: Published by the authors, 1968. Paperback book. Excellent color illustrations.

Greaser, Arlene, and Paul H. *Homespun Ceramics: A Study of Spatterware*. Allentown, Pennsylvania: Published by the authors, 1967. 3rd. ed. The illustrations in this book give a good idea of the main different types and patterns of spatter.

Godden, Geoffrey A. *Encyclopaedia of British Pottery and Porcelain Marks*. New York: Crown, 1964. The most complete book on the subject.

Chinese Porcelain

Beurdeley, Michel. *Chinese Trade Porcelain*. Rutland, Vt.: Charles E. Tuttle, 1962. This profusely illustrated book has much general information and tells the characteristics of the porcelain made for each of the countries which imported it.

Phillips, John Goldsmith. *China-Trade Porcelain: An Account of Its Historical Background, Manufacture, and Decoration and a Study of the Helena Woodworth McCann Collection*. Cambridge: Harvard Univ. Press, 1956.

Mudge, Jean McC. *Chinese Export Porcelain for the American Trade, 1785–1835*. University of Delaware, 1962. The only book on this subject and an excellent one.

Gordon, Elinor, ed. *Chinese Export Porcelain, An Historical Survey*. Anaheim, California: Main Street, 1976. The best of a selection of articles on Chinese export porcelain reprinted from back issues of the magazine *Antiques,* with an introduction by Mrs. Gordon.

Schiffer, Herbert; Peter; and Nancy. *Chinese Export Porcelain, Standard Patterns and Forms, 1780–1880*. Exton, Pennsylvania: Schiffer Publishing, 1975. These are the most readily available of the Chinese export porcelains.

French Porcelain

de Plinval de Guillebon, Régine. *Porcelain of Paris 1770–1850*. New York: Walker and Company, 1972. This book deals with the porcelain made in Paris in defiance of the royal monoply of the Sèvres factory. These hard-paste porcelains have long been lumped together under the label of "Vieux Paris", making this scholarly book very welcome.

Schleiger, Arlene. *Two Hundred Patterns of Haviland China*. Book 1, 2nd rev. ed., Omaha, 1959; Book 2, Omaha, 1957; Book 3, rev. ed., Omaha, 1962; Book 4, Omaha, 1960; Book 5, Omaha, 1974.

Young, Harriet. *Grandmother's Haviland*. Des Moines, Iowa: Wallace-Homestead Book, 1970. 2nd rev. ed.

GLASS

General

Dreppard, Carl. *ABC's of Old Glass*. New York: Award Books, 1968. A must for every collector. Our quote in the book is typical of the realism which makes this book so helpful.

American

McKearin, George S., and Helen. *American Glass*. New York: Crown, 1941. A comprehensive work on this subject. More than 300 illustrations.

__________. *Two Hundred Years of American Blown Glass*. New York: Bonanza Books, 1950.

Lee, Ruth Webb. *Early American Pressed Glass*. Wellesley Hills, Massachusetts: Lee Publications, 1931. Twice revised and enlarged. This book for years has been important to every serious collector.

__________. *Sandwich Glass*. Wellesley Hills, Massachusetts: Lee Publications, 1939.

__________. *Victorian Glass*. Wellesley Hills, Massachusetts: Lee Publications, 1944.

Metz, Alice Hulett. *Early American Pattern Glass*. Chicago: Published by author, 1958. 7th printing, 1966.

__________. *Much More Early American Pattern Glass*. Chicago: Published by author. These two books by Alice Metz do not replace Lee's books but list more patterns as research continued in this category.

Koch, Robert. *Louis C. Tiffany, Rebel in Glass*. New York: Crown, 1964–66. 2nd ed., 6th printing, 1974.

__________. *Louis C. Tiffany's Glass — Bronzes — Lamps*. New York: Crown, 1971. 4th printing, 1975.

Revi, Albert Christian. *American Art Nouveau Glass*. Camden, New Jersey: Nelson, 1968.

__________. *American Cut and Engraved Glass*. Camden, New Jersey: Nelson, 1965.

Gardner, Paul V. *The Glass of Frederick Carder*. New York: Crown, 1971. 2nd printing, 1976.

British

Hughes, G. Bernard. *English, Scottish and Irish Table Glass, From the Sixteenth Century to 1820*. New York: Bramhall House, 1954.

Beard, Geoffry. *19th Century English Cameo Glass*. Newport, Mon., England: The Ceramic Book Company, 1956.

European

Blount, Berniece, and Henry. *French Cameo Glass*. Des Moines, Iowa: Wallace-Homestead, 1968.

Grover, Ray, and Lee. *Carved and Decorated European Art Glass*. Rutland, Vermont: Charles E. Tuttle, 1970. Several hundred color plates and signatures of artists.

McClinton, Katherine M. *Lalique for Collectors*. New York: Charles Scribner's Sons, 1975.

Contemporary

Grover, Ray, and Lee. *Contemporary Art Glass*. New York: Crown, 1975.

Paperweights

Cloak, Evelyn Campbell. *Glass Paperweights of the Bergstrom Art Center*. New York: Bonanza Books, 1969. One of the finest collections in the United States. See Bergstrom Museum in Neenah, Wisconsin; also Paperweights Collectors Association in section listing some national antique collectors' associations in the United States.

Elville, E. M. *Paperweights and Other Glass Curiosities.* London: Country Life, 1961. 4th printing, 1970.

Melvin, Jean Sutherland. *American Glass Paperweights and Their Makers.* New York: Thomas A. Nelson, 1967.

Marbles

Baumann, Paul. *Collecting Antique Marbles.* Leon, Iowa: Prairie Winds Press, 1970. A pioneer book, well-written and having fine illustrations in color. Some ceramic marbles are included in this book.

Late Glass

Klamkin, Marian. *The Collector's Guide to Carnival Glass.* New York: Hawthorne Books, 1976.

_______. *The Collector's Guide to Depression Glass.* New York: Hawthorne Books, 1973.

TEXTILES

Channing, Marion L. *The Textile Tools of Colonial Homes.* Marion, Mass.: Published by author, 1969. "From Raw Materials to Finished Garments Before Mass Production in the Factories." An excellent small book, beautifully illustrated by Walter E. Channing.

Davison, Mildred, and Mayer-Thurman, Christa. *Coverlets: A Handbook on the Collection of Woven Coverlets in the Art Institute of Chicago.* Chicago: The Art Institute, 1973.

Ring, Betty, ed. *Needlework, An Historical Survey.* Main-street-Universe Books. Paperback. Selected articles from the magazine *Antiques*. A general introduction and an introduction to each section. Illustrated and indexed.

Harbeson, Georgiana Brown. *American Needlework*. New York: Coward-McCann, 1938. Bonanza edition. Probably the best single book on the subject.

Holstein, Johnathan. *American Pieced Quilts*. Washington: Smithsonian Institution, 1972.

Orlosky, Patsy, and Myra. *Quilts in America*. New York: McGraw Hill, 1974.

Safford, Carleton L., and Bishop, Robert. *American Quilts and Coverlets*. New York: Weathervane Books, 1974.

Bishop, Robert. *New Discoveries in American Quilts*. New York: Dutton, 1975. This new book contains 240 illustrations including 160 in color, documenting new finds of American quilts.

ORIENTAL RUGS AND CARPETS

Dilly, Arthur Urbane. *Oriental Rugs and Carpets*. Philadelphia: J. B. Lippincott, 1931. Revised by Maurice S. Dimand, 1957. "Herein is an interpretation — the first to be undertaken — of the spirit of rugs as revealed by the record of national personality"— from the introduction to this book.

Dimand, Dr. Maurice S. *Peasant and Nomad Rugs of Asia*. New York: Asia House Gallery, 1961. A catalogue with an introductory text by Dr. Dimand, Curator Emeritus of Near Eastern Art at the Metropolitan Museum of Art, New York.

Hawley, Walter A. *Oriental Rugs, Antique and Modern*. London: John Lane, 1913. Reissued in paperback by Dover Publications. Much information for little money.

Hubel, Reinhard G. *The Book of Carpets.* New York: Praeger, 1970.

MAPS AND PRINTS

Lister, Raymond. *How to Identify Old Maps and Globes.* Camden, Connecticut: Archon Books, 1965.

Skelton, R. A. *Maps, A Historical Survey of Their Study and Collecting.* Chicago: University of Chicago Press.

Tooley, R. V. *Maps and Map-Makers.* New York: Bonanza, 1961.

Woodward, David, ed. *Five Centuries of Map Printing.* Chicago: University of Chicago Press, 1975.

Zigrosser, Carl. *Prints and Their Creators: A World History.* New York: Crown, 1974. 2nd rev. ed. An anthology of printed pictures and introduction to the study of graphic art in the West and the East.

Zigrosser, Carl, and Gaehde, Christa M. *A Guide to the Collecting and Care of Original Prints.* New York: Crown, 1965.

Dolloff, Francis W., and Perkinson, Roy L. *How to Care for Works of Art on Paper.* Boston: Museum of Fine Arts, 1971. Written by the chief conservator and assistant conservator of the Department of Prints and Drawings of the M.F.A., this is an authoritative guide to a too little-known subject.

Middendorf, J. William, and Shadwell, Wendy J. *American Printmaking: The First 150 Years.* Washington: Smithsonian Institution, 1969.

JEWELRY

Hamlyn, Paul. *Jewelry Through the Ages.* Feltham, Middlesex, England: Hamlyn House, 1970.

Flower, Margaret. *Victorian Jewelry.* South Brunswick, New Jersey: A. S. Barnes, 1951, 1967.

Gere, Charlotte. *American and European Jewelry 1830–1914.* New York: Crown, 1975.

PEWTER

American

Montgomery, Charles F. *A History of American Pewter.* New York: Praeger, 1973. Charles Montgomery's book and Ledlie Laughlin's books on American pewter contain everything in written form a collector of this category is likely to need.

Laughlin, Ledlie Irwin. *Pewter in America: Its Makers and Their Marks.* Barre, Mass.: Barre Publishers. Reprint (2 vols. in one), 1969; vol. III, 1971.

English

Cotterelle, Howard H. *Old Pewter, It's Makers and Marks.* Rutland, Vermont: Charles E. Tuttle, 1963–1974. An account of the old pewterer and his craft in England, Scotland and Ireland.

Michaelis, Ronald F. *Antique Pewter of the British Isles.* London: G. Bell, 1955. A brief survey of what has been made in pewter in England and the British Isles from the time of Queen Elizabeth I to the reign of Queen Victoria.

Peal, Christopher A. *British Pewter and Britannia Metal.* London: John Gifford, 1971.

OTHER METALS

Kauffman, Henry J. *American Copper and Brass.* Camden, New Jersey: Thomas Nelson, 1968.

Lea, Zilla Rider, ed. *The Ornamented Tray, Two Centuries of Ornamented Trays 1720–1820.* Based on Esther Stevens Brazer's photographic collection, this book shows the development of a category that is still being made today.

Revi, Albert Christian, ed. *Spinning Wheel's Collectible Iron, Tin, Copper and Brass. Spinning Wheel Magazine,* Everybody's Press, Inc., 1974. Castle Books. Many interesting categories are represented in this book.

Kauffman, Henry J. *Early American Ironware, Cast and Wrought.* Camden, New Jersey: Thomas Nelson.

Coffin, Margaret. *The History and Folklore of American Country Tinware 1700–1900.* New York: Thomas Nelson, 1968 — Galahad Books. A very readable, well-illustrated book.

Cook, Lawrence S., ed. *Lighting in America: From Colonial Rushlights to Victorian Chandeliers.* Mainstreet paperback, 1976. The best of a selection of lighting devices reprinted from back issues of the magazine *Antiques,* with an introduction by Mr. Cooke.

Gentle, Rupert D., and Field, Rachael. *English Domestic Brass, 1680–1810.* New York: Dutton, 1975. This is an excellent (and expensive) book that is very useful in showing what desirable objects were made in this metal. With silver and pewter becoming very expensive, in the better designs, this book has added importance.

Sloan, Eric. *A Museum of Early American Tools.* New York: Funk & Wagnalls, 1964.

TOYS AND DOLLS

McClinton, Katherine M. *Antiques of American Childhood.* New York: Potter, 1970. 380 illustrations.

Coleman, Dorothy S.; Elizabeth A.; and Evelyn J. *The Collector's Encyclopedia of Dolls.* New York: Crown, 1971. 3rd printing. This book contains 2,000 illustrations and marks in color and black and white and a formidable amount of information about dolls, their makers, their clothing and their preservation.

National Collector's Associations and Clubs

These are a few of the national collector's organizations. Ask a dealer who specializes in the antiques or collectibles of your choice about other groups.

A very good way to learn about antiques is to get together interested people in your community and form your own collectors' study group.

THE QUESTERS

210 S. Quince Street
Philadelphia, Pennsylvania 19107
(215) 923-5183

"To promote, through local groups, the study and appreciation of antiques, objects of art and their historical background; to aid in the restoration of historical places through the Restoration and Preservation Fund." This is an organization for people with an active interest in antiques and the willingness to learn more about them. From the National Office you can get information about the chapter nearest you; or how to form a chapter of your own. There are many Quester chapters in the Midwest.

THE AMERICAN HISTORICAL PRINT COLLECTORS SOCIETY

Mr. Ladd MacMillan, President
P.O. Box 223
Snug Harbor Station
Duxbury, Massachusetts 12332

For information about membership, write: E. L. Newman, Secretary, P.O. Box 5122, Westport, Connecticut 06880.

AMERICAN BELL ASSOCIATION

Route 1, Box 286
Natrona Heights, Pennsylvania 15065
(412) 295-9623

Bell collectors and dealers.

NATIONAL BUTTON SOCIETY OF AMERICA

Box 116
Lamoni, Iowa 50140
(515) 784-3338

Collectors of and dealers in antique buttons.

DELTIOLOGISTS OF AMERICA (Postcard)

318 Roosevelt Avenue
Folsom, Pennsylvania 19033
(215) 532-2828

UNITED FEDERATION OF DOLL CLUBS

c/o C. L. Seidel
7720 Englewood Drive
Lincoln, Nebraska 68510

PAPERWEIGHT COLLECTORS ASSOCIATION
Paul Jokelson
P.O. Box 128
Scarsdale, New York 10583

THE PEWTER COLLECTOR'S CLUB OF AMERICA
18 East Hill Road
Torrington, Connecticut 06790

AMERICAN POLITICAL ITEM COLLECTORS
66 Golf Street
Newington, Connecticut 06111
(203) 666-3892

**NATIONAL ASSOCIATION OF
FRIENDS OF RARE PORCELAIN**
1911 Boardwalk
Atlantic City, New Jersey 08401
(609) 344-1128

THE SPOONER
Route 1, Box 49
Shullsburg, Wisconsin 53586
(608) 965-3179

Collectors of souvenir spoons.

**NATIONAL ASSOCIATION OF
WATCH AND CLOCK COLLECTORS**
P.O. Box 33
Columbia, Pennsylvania 17512
(717) 684-8261